Words They Lived By

Colonial New England Speech, Then and Now

by

Joan P. Bines

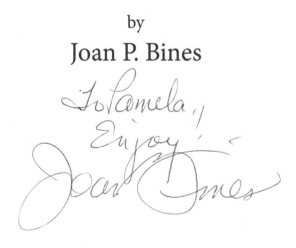

Published & distributed by:

Eye of the Beholder

in association with:

IBJ Book Publishing

41 E. Washington St., Suite 200

Indianapolis, IN 46204

www.ibjbp.com

ISBN 978-1-934922-89-7

First Edition

Library of Congress Control Number: 2013933081

Printed in the United States of America

All photos courtesy of GBT (Golden Ball Tavern) unless otherwise noted.

ACKNOWLEDGEMENTS

*W*ords *They Lived By* could not have been written without the information and insights gleaned from the extensive body of writing by eighteenth and nineteenth century participants and observers, and by modern-day historians, scholars, and specialists whose books are listed in full in the bibliography. I invite and urge readers to make their own journey of discovery in these authors' works. I also greatly appreciate the support of the Trustees and Tavernkeepers of the Golden Ball Tavern Museum, a unique

The Golden Ball Tavern. A 1992 print by Anne Bell Robb, Sherborn, Massachusetts.

archaeological and historical museum in Weston, Massachusetts, steeped in colonial history with buildings, artifacts, archives and library that have informed every aspect of this book. I owe a debt of gratitude to Edward Maeder, world-renowned expert in textile and costume, Barbara Provest, expert in colonial weaving, and Stephanie Smith, expert in colonial dress, who generously shared their knowledge; to the Spellman Museum of Stamps and Postal History's Director Henry Lucas and Curator George Norton who shared a treasure of United States postage stamps, as well as their expertise; to Christopher Anderson, colonial furniture maker, who shared his knowledge of the period and allowed me to photograph his beautiful Brown Bess and British sword; and to colonial re-enactor, Simon Rubenstein, who allowed me to photograph his replica colonial hatchet.

I am indebted to Linda Wiseman who time and again by word and deed helped me improve the book and to Pamela Bailey Powers who read the work once as a writer and twice as an artist, and who, when I was struggling to find illustrations, said, "Joan, you are a photographer. Go take the pictures." I thank my editor, Francie King (HistoryKeep.com) whose fine skills and love of language greatly enhanced the project. I also thank Rachel Max, Dan Alden, Theresa Cader, Peter and Lyn Lord, Susan Bennett, Pam Fox, and Robert A. Erbetta for their most useful suggestions; and Dorothea Waterbury and John G. Brooks (of blessed memory) and Sarah Brooks and Cate MacKinnon, for being my cheerleaders and sounding boards over the years.

A special thank you goes to the gifted team of Pat Keiffner, Jodi Belcher, Mike Button and Helen O'Guinn at IBJ Book Publishing who, with great talent and much patience, took the raw material and adeptly worked it into a polished book.

Above all, I thank my husband, Harvey Bines, for his careful reading of the manuscript, and our family, Alexandra Jacobs, Jonathan, Josie, and Sy Bines; Audrey, Joel, Lily, Gabe, and Estelle Bines; Susanne, Zach, Leah, and Caroline Hafer; and Benjamin Bines for their suggestions, their loving support, and their wholehearted belief in the project.

Author's Note:
Except where indicated, I photographed the illustrations in the book from the vast collection at the Golden Ball Tavern Museum where I have been fortunate to serve as the director for many, many years. The picture of the *Mayflower* and the picture of the stage-coach are from the New York Public Library's Mid-Manhattan branch which has a superb picture collection; the United States postage stamps are courtesy of the Spellman Museum of Stamps and Postal History in Weston, Massachusetts; the picture of tenterhooks is from J. Edwards; and the photographs of the Minuteman statue and the gravestone I took in Lexington, Massachusetts, a town rich in colonial history.

Please be aware, in colonial days the letter *s* was printed as an *f* when it came in the middle, and often at the beginning, of a printed word.

CONTENTS

THE FIRST SETTLERS

The small band of Pilgrims who settled in Plymouth Colony in the 1620s, and the more than 20,000 Puritans who crossed the ocean soon after them in the Great Migration to settle in the Massachusetts Bay Colony and beyond, were already steeped in the language, life ways, and customs of other

The Mayflower at Sea. *Illustration from* Pioneers in the Settlement of America, *1876.*

lands, predominantly those of England. In this new world, however, they encountered a unique set of political, social, and cultural challenges as they worked to build homes, raise families, make a living, and create religious and governing organizations to serve their needs.

Their first job was to build shelters and eke out a meager subsistence for themselves and their families. Toward that end, they came remarkably well prepared. This ditty suggests that many of the men who came to New England in the great migration were skilled craftsmen:

> Tom Taylor is prepared,
> And th' Smith as black as a coal;
> Ralph Cobler too with us will go.
> For he regards his soul;
> The Weaver, honest Simon …
> Professeth to come after.[1]

And the women had successfully managed households and raised children before they sailed to New England.

What bound the early settlers together and set the tone for their lives was their faith. They had left the comforts of the known to come to a wilderness where they hoped to practice their Pilgrim and Puritan religious beliefs in peace. Although some wanted to build a bible commonwealth and spread their religious convictions to the Indians, most came to practice personal piety in a community of believers. They built houses close together and close to the meetinghouse (their church). Males who met the strict religious requirements to be accepted into church membership selected their town's preacher and magistrates and helped decide the rules that the entire community lived by. Having committed a radical act by coming to New England, once here, they established a participatory, responsible, orderly, neighborly, stable way of life.

On the other hand, their motivation for transporting themselves to the New World was to live in pursuit of religious purity, to incorporate their religious and moral beliefs into every aspect of their daily lives. For many years, then, they lived in a theocracy that brooked little dissent. They were superstitious, rigid, and intolerant. They burned witches; they whipped and publicly humiliated those judged to have violated their strict moral rules; and they persecuted Quakers and expelled dissenters such as Roger Williams and Anne Hutchinson. They had Negro and Indian slaves and participated in the slave trade. While they accepted women into church membership, they denied them any participation in church or town governance.

The rigidity and intolerance was not unusual in civilized societies in those days, but the New England Puritan belief in and promotion of education was unusual. In 1647, believing that ignorance of the Bible benefited "that old deluder, Satan," Massachusetts legislated that every town of fifty families establish and keep a common school, and, for towns of more than 100, a Latin school—Boston Latin School was established in 1635—to prepare young men to attend college—Harvard College was established in 1636—where they were to study to become ministers. It became the duty of the towns to teach children to read, an act that in turn became an important dynamic promoting progress.

The great majority of men and women who came after the Puritans settled into the ordered existence that they found in place in New England. Over time, laws were allowed to adapt, gradually becoming more secular and enabling the community to prosper. By the time of the Revolutionary War, the colonists had succeeded in creating functioning institutions, a thriving economy, and a vibrant social, political, and religious life that would contribute greatly to the founding of the new republic.

Just as their society and government evolved, so too did their language. The colonists brought words with them but subtly changed or adapted their meanings. They incorporated words from other countries and peoples. They created words. And all were aimed at giving voice to what was happening around them. By focusing on words and phrases they used then—words and phrases that we still use today—we can peek into their lives and watch as Goodwife Jones, or "Goody" Jones as she would have been called, went about the daily chores of wife and mother. We can see her yeoman farmer husband, Goodman Jones, clear the land, plant the crops, and perhaps visit the local tavern to imbibe a tankard of ale, visit, and share conversation over the latest news brought by a traveler or post rider staying at the inn. We can become more acquainted with how their society developed and changed, and we can enjoy knowing the early history of words we currently use.

Share with me these words that served in colonial days and that, evolving in time, continue to serve.

THE FIRST SETTLERS
Chapter Notes:

1   Fischer, *Albion's Seed*, 30.

MEN AND WORK

*I*n the 1840s Henry David Thoreau wrote this evocative description of the colonists' labor:[1]

> *Some spring the white man came, built him a house, and made a clearing here, letting in the sun, dried up a farm, piled up the old grey stones in fences, cut down the pines around his dwelling, planted orchard seeds brought from the old country, and persuaded the civil appletree to blossom next to the wild pine and juniper, shedding its perfume in the wilderness. Their old stocks still remain. He culled the graceful elm from out the woods and from the river-side, and so refined and smoothed his village plot. He rudely bridged the stream, and drove his team afield into the river meadows, cut the wild grass, and laid bare the homes of beaver, otter, muskrat, and with the whetting of his scythe scared off the deer and bear. He set up a mill, and fields of English grain sprang in the virgin soil. And with his grain he scattered the seeds of the dandelion and the wild trefoil over the meadows, mingling his English flowers with the wild native ones. The bristling burdock, the sweet-scented catnip, and the humble yarrow planted themselves along his woodland road, they too seeking "freedom to worship God" in their way. And thus he plants a town.[1]*

In addition to the endless demands of farming, men participated in religious and political life, and served in the local militia. They engaged in a wide variety of occupations from blacksmithing to baking, from silversmithing to tailoring, from tavern keeping to store keeping, from cabinetmaking to cordwaining (shoemaking), from barbering to lawyering, from shipbuilding to fishing, from wigmaking to schoolteaching.

Gentleman

—Then

*A*lthough colonial society eschewed noble titles and coats of arms, it did make social distinctions, as John Adams noted:

> *Perhaps it may be said in America we have no distinctions of ranks ... but have we not laborers, yeomen, gentlemen, esquires, honorable gentlemen, and excellent gentlemen?*[2]

New Englanders took these distinctions seriously showing great respect for **gentlemen**, whom they considered their betters.

Unlike in England, a man could advance from the social level of yeoman (one who owned his property outright) or artisan or merchant to that of gentleman with a favorable change in fortune if he possessed the other requisite qualities. A gentleman was presumed to have manners, refinement, intelligence, education, and moral character. He and his fellow gentlemen held themselves to a high standard of both social and civic behavior. He also had the disposition, and the duty as a gentleman, to assume public responsibilities. In the mid-1700s, Paul Revere worked as a mechanic—a silversmith—but was socially accorded the title of gentleman by his fellow Bostonians. By his own definition, a gentleman was a man of character, a man who "respects his own credit."[3]

A colonial gentleman and his family. Detail from a colonial revival (late 1800s) etching entitled Forgiven *by Charles Steele.*

In the early days, only gentlemen and their families were entitled to special considerations, such as permission to wear lace or other refinements of dress. People of lesser rank were expected to curtsey or bow to them. They alone received exemption from the most common form of punishment. A 1641 Massachusetts decree held:

> *Nor shall any true gentleman nor any man equal to a gentleman be punished by whipping.*[4]

This was a prized dispensation. One Boston student wrote in 1771 of the public punishment of wrongdoers:

> *The large whipping-post painted red stood*
> *conspicuously and prominently in the most*
> *public street in the town. It was placed in*
> *State Street directly under the windows of*
> *a great writing school which I frequented,*
> *and from them the scholars were indulged*
> *in the spectacle of all kinds of punishment*
> *suited to harden their hearts and brutalize*
> *their feelings.*[5]

The work of a gentleman.

Through the years, though the habit of deference did not totally disappear, it certainly declined. During the American Revolution, British soldier Thomas Anburey stopped at a tavern with some of his fellow soldiers, one of whom was a nobleman. There he encountered a group of women who begged to meet the aristocrat. Having done so, and having been singularly unimpressed, one of the women lifted up her hands and eyes to heaven, and with great astonishment exclaimed, "Well, for my part, if that be a Lord, I never desire to see any other Lord but the Lord Jehovah," and promptly left the room.[6]

Now

A **gentleman** is a man whose conduct in his social dealings is presumed to embody ethical and personal standards of behavior, and the degree to which the word conveys honor is determined as much by the dignity of the speaker as by the conduct of the object.

Huckster

Then

*H*ucksters, hawkers, and peddlers were entrepreneurial young men who sold their goods on foot or from carts pulled along town streets, back roads, and rural trails and byways. Loaded down with his goods, the peddler sold, among other things, pots and pans, needles and thread, pins and buttons, axes and nails, lace and ribbon, and even spices and books.

These were items much needed or wanted by the townspeople, farmers, and housewives who welcomed the itinerant peddlers as much for the gossip, news, and details of the latest fashions as for the goods and they brought.

At times the hucksters got together to set up a number of booths or stalls in open fields—called huxter shops—to display their wares. Some hucksters, hoping to expand their business, also sold medicines and entertainment, evidenced by a 1773 Connecticut law that prohibited these dispensers of medical treatments from

> publickly advertising and giving notice of their skill and ability to cure diseases, and the erecting publick stages and places from whence to declaim and harangue the people on the virtue and efficacy of their medicines, or to exhibit by themselves or their dependents any plays, tricks, juggling or unprofitable feats of uncommon dexterity and agility of body, [which] tends to draw together great numbers of people, to the corruption of manners, promoting of idleness, and the determinant [sic] of good order and religion ... [7]

Now

A **huckster** is a person who tries to use his charms and salesmanship to sell someone something that the buyer does not need or something of inferior quality. The word has taken on a singularly pejorative meaning. We can see a shift in the connotation of the word even in the colonial period.

Logrolling
—*Then*

A **logrolling** was a community get-together for mutual assistance, a chance for generous cooperation. When a new settler came, he had to build a home for his family. The men of the community would come together to help him clear his building site of trees. They might also join together for stump-pullings, house or barn raisings, and stone pilings. At the end of these endeavors, neighbors would socialize and share the meal prepared by wives and sweethearts.

Logrolling is the exchange of favors or votes by politicians so that each gets his or her pet project funded. The term is also used for an act of mutual assistance, or mutual back scratching.

Lot

Then

*T*he term **lot** for a piece of land may have come from the Pilgrims' and Puritans' practice of drawing lots to determine the parcel of land granted each family in the colony. At first, the Plymouth settlers tried to farm the land communally. Finding this system demoralizing rather than productive, they chose to divide the common land and cattle among the families, with each being given an allotted portion. It has been suggested, most likely apocryphally, that, following the New Testament example of choosing the twelfth apostle by lot, Puritan families' names were drawn in the same way, and each family selected its "lot" of land as its name was drawn.[8] More likely, the term derived from the fact that in the towns in New England in the early years, each of the eligible inhabitants was allotted his share of the common meadow and upland, thus receiving his lot. The word also signified a large quantity of something.

Now

A **lot** is a piece of land with set boundaries as well as any large quantity of something. It also is a term for a person's portion or "lot" in life.

Macaroni

Then

*I*n the mid to late 1700s, **macaroni** was the name given to a dandy, a man excessively interested in his clothing and appearance and therefore thought of as vain. It was also a slang term for a fancy wig or something in high fashion. The term derived from the name of a social club in England. The club's members, who had made the "grand tour" of the Continent, put on the airs and mannerisms of Europeans. Since macaroni was a pasta eaten in Italy but not well known in England, the members elected to call their association The Macaroni Club thereby showing off their cosmopolitan refinement.

A "macaroni" gentleman depicted in a reverse-painting-on-glass courting mirror. Notice the feather in his cap.

William Ellery, a member of the Continental Congress from Rhode Island, noted in his diary in November 1777, that at one tavern, he and his fellow travelers enjoyed

> the Musick of the Spinning Wheel, and Wool-Cards and
> the Sounds of the Shoemaker's Hammer ... that might be
> disagreeable to your delicate Macaroni Gentry ... [9]

From the days of the French and Indian War (1754-1763), the British had mocked the colonial New Englanders, nicknamed Yankees, as *doodles*—rubes and bumpkins—making fun of their pretension to refinement. They sang:

> Yankee Doodle went to town
> A-riding on a pony,
> Stuck a feather in his cap
> And called it macaroni.

But at the start of the Revolutionary War the tables were turned. Thomas Anburey, in his *Eyewitness Accounts of the American Revolution*, wrote in November 1777 of the name Yankee and of the song "Yankee Doodle":

> The name has been more prevalent since the commencement
> of hostilities; the [British] soldiery at Boston used it as a term
> of reproach; but after the affair of Bunker's Hill, the Americans
> gloried in it. Yankee-doodle, is now their pœan, a favorite
> of favorites, played in their army, esteemed as warlike as the
> Grenadier's March—it is the lover's spell, the nurse's lullaby. After

> *our [the British] rapid successes, we held the Yankees in great*
> *contempt; but it was not a little mortifying to hear them play this*
> *tune, when their army marched down to our surrender.*[10]

Now

Macaroni is a form of pasta commonly eaten with butter or cheese (or both). The word no longer has any association with fashion or vanity. Indeed, when used metaphorically, it implies that the object is common, not fashionable.

Manure

Then

The verb **manure** derived from the French word *mainouverer* meaning *worked by hand*. In colonial days, to manure meant to work the field to receive the fertilizer, or to fertilize. Timothy Dwight, a minister and later president of Yale, observed during his travels in New England:

> *Fields manured with the whitefish have yielded wheat,*
> *universally, in great abundance, and with almost absolute*
> *certainty.*[11]

Now

Manure refers to the organic fertilizer itself and has almost entirely taken on the meaning of the most common organic fertilizer, dung from horses or cattle.

Mechanic

Then

In colonial days, a **mechanic** was a man who made things with his hands. Just as sellers of many different goods were called merchants, skilled craftsmen—silversmiths, goldsmiths, shipbuilders, cabinetmakers, furniture makers, and blacksmiths—were called mechanics and were as well respected for their skills as for their products. Mechanics and freemen, both somewhat lower in the social scale than gentlemen, nevertheless were important participants in the political as well as the commercial life of their communities. Paul Revere wrote:

> *In the Fall of 1774 and Winter of 1775 I was one of upwards of thirty, chiefly mechanics, who formed ourselves into a committee for the purpose of watching the movements of the British soldiers, and gaining every intelligence of the movements of the Tories.*[12]

The term mechanic connoted a lesser level of education and social standing than that of gentleman. One Loyalist in Concord in the 1770s was amazed to hear a Whig furniture-maker speak eloquently in debate with the leading Loyalist lawyer. Demanding to know the identity of the speaker, the Loyalist listener was told that the speaker was a mechanic named Joseph Hosmer. How then was the man able to speak "such pure English," the Loyalist wondered?[13]

Now

The term is less general, excluding those expert in crafts. A **mechanic** is one skilled with machines and tools—making, using, and repairing them. Today's mechanics work on cars, planes, and small engines such as lawnmowers and air conditioners. The implication respecting their command of English expression yet persists.

Plantation
Then

A **plantation** in colonial days in New England meant a settlement or a planted area, hence the name Plymouth Plantation. A 1635 law of the Massachusetts Bay Colony required that

> *no dwelling house shall be built above half a mile from the meeting house in any new plantation ... without leave from the*

Court, except mill houses & farm houses of such as have their dwelling houses in some town.[14]

To preserve the peace of the community, Dorchester enacted a ruling in 1634:

No man within the Plantation shall sell his house or lott to any man without the Plantation whome they shall dislike of.[15]

Now

A **plantation** is a large estate on which the owner grows cash crops such as sugar cane, indigo, rice, cotton, or tobacco for market using the labor of hired workers or, before the abolition of slavery, slaves. Particularly in the colonial South, use of the word lost its communal connotation. In New England and the Northeast, as industrialization displaced agriculture and large tracts of land close to towns were no longer farmed as they had been, the historic use of the word lost its utility. Because of the association of the word plantation with antebellum slavery, use of this word, especially as an adjective, has long carried, and still carries disdain, if not outright disapproval.

Pocketbook

Then

*I*n colonial days, a **pocketbook** was a case, carried in a man's pocket, containing two hinged compartments; when it was opened, it resembled a book. The pocketbook served a practical purpose: to carry the paper money of the day along with important documents and bills.

During the Revolutionary War, Thomas Anburey wrote movingly of a mother in deep distress who asked some passing British soldiers if they had seen her missing son:

LOST by the subscriber, last evening, between the meeting house in Cambridge and Kent's tavern in Dorchester, a Leather Pocket Book containing a number of notes of hand to great value, with other papers of importance ; together with about 5 or 6 pounds L. M. in cash — Whoever will return the pocket book and contents to the printer or subscriber, shall be entitled to the cash with thanks
Dec 10. JOSEPH P. PALMER.

Advertisement for a lost pocketbook in the Boston Gazette and Country Journal, *December 18, 1775.*

> *She then enquired about his pocket-book, and if any of his papers were safe, as some related to his estates, and if any of the soldiers had got his watch; if she could but obtain that in remembrance of her dear, dear son, she should be happy.* [16]

Frequently covered in elaborate needlework, a pocketbook also served an aesthetic purpose as a status symbol showing off the level of sewing skill and artistry that a man's wife had attained and could lavish on him. Additionally, men could purchase pocketbooks as shown by this advertisement in the *Boston Gazette*, June 13, 1763:

> *Just Imported from London, and to be sold by John Perkins, at his shop in Union Street, nearly opposite to Deacon Grant's ... All kinds of stationary ware, writing, printing, ... Spanish pocketbooks, pocket ivory memorandum books ... .* [17]

Now

Today's **pocketbook** is a purse carried mainly by women (though becoming more popular among urban men) to hold their wallets, combs, lipsticks, and other necessities.

Tinker

Then

*I*n the 1700s when imported tin began to be used for making candlesticks, basins, plates, lanterns, pots, and such, the **tinkers'** trade was born in the colonies. Tinware was popular because it was cheaper than silverware. The tinker was a traveling workman who mended tinware and tin pots. In 1742, the master of a runaway indentured servant advertised, "He had also a spoon and Dial Mould and other Tinker's Tools."[18]

Tin lantern.

Now

Tinker is a verb meaning to use spare time to play or work with or repair machine parts or mechanical objects. One can also tinker in the sense of fine tuning, as in tinkering with a plan to improve it or make it better fit its objectives.

Tinker's damn (or dam)
Then

The itinerant colonial tinker had a reputation for using profane language. The cursing was so frequent that people became immune to its effect, hence the meaninglessness of a **tinker's damn**. Another possible origin of the phrase has it that the tinker used a tiny rolled up ball of bread or clay, a dam, to hold the flowing solder in place in the tinware he was mending. When the solder had set, the tinker discarded the worthless tinker's dam.

Now

A **tinker's dam** is a meaningless amount. If you don't give a tinker's dam, you don't care in the least.

Truck
Then

The word **truck** referred to an exchange of wares or any goods used for trade, such as furs, cloth, knives, scissors, pots and pans, butter, cheeses, and even bullets. Since coin was scarce in the colonies, truck was commonly used as payment for goods and services. One woman advertised in 1751 that she would sell her goods "for cash or truck that will answer …"[19] From the 1780s on, truck included the vegetables grown in gardens by farmers and their wives and taken for sale to the local markets. The truck farm provided the farmer and his family with goods to barter for necessities and luxuries the farm did not produce.

Long before the automotive truck was invented, truck was also the word for a type of low carriage having a single axel that rolled upon circular pieces of wood called trucks. These trucks carried heavy loads and were pulled by two horses harnessed in tandem.

The Town of Boston adopted a bylaw in 1727 prohibiting trucks "whose Sides exceed the length of Sixteen Feet" or that was pulled by "more than Two Horses at a Time" from being driven through the lanes or streets of the city.[20] In 1873 in *Landmarks and Historic Personages of Boston*, Samuel Adams Drake lamented the disappearance of the colonial trucks for with them went

> *that distinctive body of men, the 'Boston Truckmen,' who once formed a leading and attractive feature of our public processions, with their white frocks and black hats, mounted with their magnificent truck-horses.*[21]

Trucks, tumbrels, carts, wheelbarrows, and handbarrows were all used for carrying goods and materials.

Now

A **truck** is a heavy vehicle built to haul goods. A truck farm is a farm that produces vegetables to be sold at a nearby market or perhaps even from the farmer's truck.

Wallet

Then

A **wallet** was the colonial term for a type of knapsack used to hold food, clothing, and such provisions as might be needed for a trip. On September 2, 1774, the morning after commander of British forces in America, General Thomas Gage sent soldiers to capture the patriot ammunition stored in the provincial powder house near Boston, a traveler named McNeil wrote of the people's response:

> *All along [the road] were armed men rushing forward—some on foot, some on horseback. At every house women and children [were] making cartridges, running bullets, making **wallets**, baking biscuits, crying and bemoaning and at the same time animating their husbands and sons to fight for their liberties, though not knowing whether they should ever see them again.*[22]

Now

Today's **wallet** is a billfold, a small folded case for a pocket or purse, usually made of leather or fabric in which money, pictures, and cards are kept.

MEN AND WORK
Chapter Notes:

1   Thoreau, 56-57.

2   Fischer, *Albion's Seed*, 179.

3   Fischer, *Paul Revere's Ride*, 17.

4   Lederer, Jr., *Colonial American English*, 102.

5   *Diary of Anna Green Winslow*, 111.

6   Anburey, *Travels*, vol. 2, 52-53.

7   Benes, "Itinerant Entertainers," 119.

8   De Vere, *Americanism*, 182. Devere continues: "the firm belief of the Puritans in a special providence watching over them and their interests made them continually resort to this manner of distributing lands or other articles of value, held heretofore in common, and thus the term *lots* soon came to designate any great quantity."

9   Ellery, 323.

10   Anburey, *Travels*, vol. 2, 50-51.

11   Dwight, *Travel*, vol. II, 237.

12   Fischer, *Paul Revere's Ride*, 51.

13   Fischer, *Paul Revere's Ride*, 205-6.

14   Fischer, *Albion's Seed*, 181.

15   Earle, *Home Life*, 157.

16   Anburey, *Travels*, vol. 2, 209.

17   Dow, *Arts and Crafts*, 282.

18   Dow, *Arts and Crafts*, 195.

19   Dexter, 32.

20   Dow, *Arts and Crafts*, 286.

21   Dow, *Every Day Life*, 65.

22   Fischer, *Paul Revere's Ride*, 46.

WOMEN AND WORK

Most colonial women worked from sunup to sundown, bearing and raising children, carding wool, combing flax, spinning, knitting, sewing, quilting, cooking, baking, butchering, washing, gardening, and making cider, cheeses, butter, candles, and soap. They were the midwives, the herbalists, the nurses. Even unmarried women, though rare in a society that valued marriage and home above all, played their role in performing these tasks for the family.

Women had to do the daily magic of turning raw material into food for the table, clothing and linens for the family, beer and cider for the mugs. The wife of a Dover, New Hampshire, minister only slightly exaggerated when she wrote:

> Up in the morning I must rise
> Before I've time to rub my eyes.
> With half-pin'd gown, unbuckled shoe,
> I hast to milk my lowing cow.
> But, Oh! It makes my heart to ake,
> I have no bread till I can bake,
> And then, alas! It makes me sputter,
> For I must churn or have no butter.
> The hogs with swill too I must serve;
> For hogs must eat or men will starve … .
> Corn must be husk'd, and pork be kill'd,
> The house with all confusion fill'd.
> O could you see the grand display
> Upon our annual butchering day,—
> See me look like ten thousand sluts,
> My kitchen spread with grease & guts … [1]

It fell to the women to make sure that there was fire in the great fireplace to cook meals. A young Watertown girl remembered her mother getting up one morning early, coming into the kitchen and finding her fire gone out. Her daughter described it thus:

> *Our custom then was to rake up the fire carefully at night under*
> *the ashes so as to preserve it in case of sickness in the night or*
> *convenience for kindling the fire in the morning. Lucifer matches*
> *were not yet invented, and, to save herself the trouble of striking*
> *fire in a tinderbox, she awoke little George, gave him a pair of*
> *small light tongs and bid him run to the next neighbor's house in*
> *sight, and get a coal of fire … .*[2]

Despite the importance of their contributions, wives were clearly believed
to be subservient to their husbands. In May 1776, Abigail Adams spoke
candidly to her husband, John, about the risks of this attitude:

> *I can not say that I think you very generous to the Ladies,*
> *for whilst you are proclaiming peace and good will to Men,*
> *Emancipating all Nations, you insist upon retaining an absolute*
> *power over Wives. But you must remember that Arbitary [sic]*
> *power is like most other things which are very hard, very liable*
> *to be broken—and notwithstanding all your wise Laws and*
> *Maxims we have it in our power not only to free ourselves but*
> *to subdue our Masters, and without violence throw both your*
> *natural and legal authority at our feet … .*[3]

Still, though they could not vote or hold office, women were admitted to full
church membership and were generally protected by the Puritan belief in
family, in loving partnership between a man and a woman, and in spiritual
equality, as well as by laws that helped safeguard them from the tyranny
of their husbands, including the right to divorce. Trying to reconcile the
apparent discrepancy in the relations between man and wife, one minister
wrote somewhat convolutedly:

> *Of all the orders which are unequals, these do come nearest to*
> *an Equality, and in several respects they stand upon an even*
> *ground. These two do make a pair, which infers so far a parity.*[4]

Despite the endless work and the inequalities, the majority of women led
lives like those of their husbands, full and busy, productive and necessary to
the wellbeing of their families and their community.

Distaff

The **distaff** was (and still is) the staff-like part of the small flax spinning wheel over which the combed flax fiber was spread as an aid for the spinner as she pulled out strands to be twisted and spun into linen thread. Since the women of the family did most of the spinning, the words "distaff side" adhered to them. The distaff was as firmly associated with female work as the plough with male work in colonial society.

The distaff of a flax wheel.

One son lovingly recalled his mother's work with this poem:

> *The boys dressed the flax, the girls spun the tow,*
> *The music of mother's footwheel was not slow.*
> *The flax on the bended pine distaff was spread,*
> *With squash shell of water to moisten the thread.*
> *Such were the pianos our mothers did keep*
> *Which they played on while spinning their children to sleep.*
> *My mother I'm sure must have borne off the medal,*
> *For she always was placing her foot on the pedal.*
> *The warp and the filling were piled in the room,*
> *Till the web was completed and fit for the loom.*
> *Then labor was pleasure, and industry smiled,*
> *And the wheel and the loom every trouble beguiled,*
> *And there at the distaff the good wives were made.*
> *Thus Solomon's precepts were fully obeyed.*[5]

Now

Distaff or **distaff side** refers to girls and women or to work considered to be women's work. Some men (brave or benighted!) might say that they happily leave the cooking to the "distaff side." As early as 1806, in his *A Compendious Dictionary of the English Language*, the first dictionary of American words, Noah Webster defined distaff as both a staff used in spinning and as a woman.

Dyed in the wool
—*Then*

Woolen fleece was shorn from sheep, washed, and combed with wool combs for worsted spinning or hand cards for woolen spinning. Then, if it was to be dyed, it was either **dyed in the wool** before being spun into yarn or dyed after it was spun. If she did not wish to dye it herself, the housewife might take her yarn to a professional dyer such as Edward Carter who offered himself in 1735 as a

> *Silk Dyer and Scowrer from London, at the Rainbow and blue Hand in Wing's Lane Boston: Dyes and Scowers all sorts of Brocades, Velvets, Silks, Stuffs, Linnen and Woolen, as in his former Advertisements, with Care and expedition.*[6]

Another dyer, Alexander Fleming, placed this advertisement in the *Boston Gazette and Country Journal* in 1754:

> *Dyer, lately from Great Britain … who can dye all sorts of Colours, after the best Manner and cheapest Rate, vis. Scarletts, Crimsons, Pinks, Purples, Straws, Wine Colours, Sea-Greens, Saxon ditto, common Blues, shearing, dressing and watering of cloths: Also he can dye linnen Yarn either red, blue, green, yellow or cloth colors, and all Colours on silks, and cleaning of Cloths.*[7]

Many in colonial days must have learned what Daniel Webster discovered in the early 1800s, that even dyed-in-the-wool material would not hold its color if it was not well rinsed and if a good mordant was not used to set the dye before it was woven. Caught out in the rain on horseback, he

> *had the blues for many days after his arrival … because a drenching rain had washed the indigo from his new suit dyed in*

A dye pot with wool.

the wool at home, into his skin, coloring it deeply, darkly, beautifully blue.[8]

Now

Dyed in the wool refers to the quality of a person's deep commitment to a cause, a commitment not readily altered.

Heckle

—Then

To **heckle,** in making linen, was to pull the flax fibers firmly and repeatedly across parallel rows of coarse, medium, and then fine metal spikes set into wooden boards called heckles, hackles, or hetchels. Heckling was an important step in the process of preparing flax for spinning. It was done to straighten the fibers to make them easier to spin as well as to remove any short-fibered tow that would adversely affect the quality of the linen thread. The long, silky fibers that remained would be placed upon the distaff to be spun into linen thread.

Various sized heckles.

In adherence with the law of the Massachusetts General Court from 1640 to 1656, nearly every Massachusetts household grew a patch of flax whose fiber could be woven into linen cloth to make clothing and linens. To prepare the flax plant for spinning, the men of the family would first have had to *rett* (use water to break down the tough outer coating of the flax stem), *break* (use a flax break to crush the woody outer fiber), and *scutch* (use a scutching board to scrape off the outer woody part to release the desired flax fibers within). Only then would they pull the flax fibers through heckles to produce the long, smooth, warm pale yellow fiber. A young woman with long light-blond tresses might be said to be flaxen haired.

Now

To **heckle** means to badger, annoy, and harass a speaker with barbed questions, taunts, and shouts. Some say that this meaning came about because in the early 1900s, a group of flax hecklers in Scotland, who paid close attention to the news of the day, participated vociferously and argumentatively in town politics.

Homespun
—*Then*

*H*omespun was the cloth woven and sewn from homespun yarn and used by the early colonial housewife to make her family's simple clothing such as shirts, shifts, and aprons. As a vast selection of imported worsteds, silks, calamancos, broadcloths, harrateens, velvets, corduroys, damasks, linen, and plate- and block-printed or patterned cottons were

the SEAMSTRESS

for INDEPENDENCE USA 13c

imported into the colonies from Britain, colonial families bought these materials to sew themselves or have their seamstresses and mantua makers make skirts, gowns, cloaks, and hoods for the girls and women, and their tailors make breeches, waistcoats, and jackets for the men. Women who used imported cloth might still use their homespun thread and cloth as well as other family products—cheeses, butter, and eggs—to barter for the finer materials and clothing and for other goods.

The word *homespun* eventually took on a pejorative sense among the wealthier and more fashionable who felt it denoted "rustic." Then in the 1760s and 1770s, when the colonists' anger was kindled against the British and all things made in or bought from Britain, homespun cloth gained a virtuous and patriotic aura. Women in many of the colonies joined groups called Daughters of Liberty, bringing their spinning wheels down from the garret and vowing to wear nothing but homespun. The *Massachusetts Gazette* in 1767 encouraged:

> *Young ladies in town and those that live round*
> *Let a friend at this season advise you.*
> *Since money's so scarce and times growing worse,*

Strange things may soon hap and surprise you.
First then throw aside your high top knots of pride
Wear none but your own country linen.
Of economy boast. Let your pride be the most
To show cloaths of your own make and spinning.
What if homespun they say is not quite so gay
As brocades, yet be not in a passion,
For when once it is known this is much wore in town,
One and all will cry out 'Tis the fashion.
And as one and all agree that you'll not married be
To such as will wear London factory
But at first sight refuse, till e'en such you do choose
As encourage our own manufactory.[9]

Abigail Adams gave moving testimony to her own patriotic efforts. In April of 1777, she wrote to her husband John, who was attending the Continental Congress in Philadelphia:

I seek wool and flax and can work willingly with my Hands, and tho my Household are not cloathed with fine linen nor scarlet, they are cloathed with what is perhaps full as Honorary, the plain and decent manufactory of my own family, and tho I do not abound, I am not in want.[10]

British soldiers are said to have insultingly named the colonial army the Homespuns, implying that they were rude rustics.

Now

Homespun still means made at home or made of homemade cloth. It also connotes something worthy as well as something unpretentious. After the American Revolution, with the vastly increased availability of fine imported materials—Italian and Chinese silks, French prints, Russian linens—together with the availability and low prices of American machine-made materials, especially cotton, homespun cloth largely fell out of use.

Quilt

Then

*I*n colonial days, a **quilt** could refer to a petticoat quilted in silk or glazed wool called calamanco, as well as to a bedcover. The *Boston News-Letter* in January 1761 included this notice:

> *Barnabas Binney imported from London and had on sale at his house in Summer Street: — Newly made black, pink, blue, and green calamanco quilted petticoats.*[11]

The quilting stitched together a layer of padding between two layers of material, producing a piece that was both decorative and warm. Many women stitched their own quilts, both petticoats and bedcovers, taking pride in the design and workmanship.

Hand-stitched quilt with a line of backing showing.

They sometimes worked alone, but more frequently they worked together with a group of friends or relatives for an afternoon or sometimes for up to a week for what was called a quilting party or just a quilting. These gatherings, formal or informal, provided a welcome social break. Women could come together to talk and exchange news and gossip while they worked. Not until the late nineteenth century were these gatherings called quilting bees, but whatever the name, they partook of all the welcome socializing. A few were even followed by entertainment. In a 1774 entry, one diarist noted that a Mrs. Parker hosted a quilting "with about 20 Girls & about as many young men at Evening," and the Parkers had another quilt completed followed by "a fine Dance at night [with] a Fiddle."[12]

Now

A **quilt** is a bedcover made in three layers—a decorative top, a layer of batting, and a plain lower layer of fabric all stitched together with the stitching forming an attractive pattern.

Shuttle
—Then

The **shuttle** was the weaver's instrument for carrying the bobbin, wound with thread, back and forth repeatedly across the loom between the lifted arrangements of warp threads—the sheds. By altering which threads were lifted on any given pass of the shuttle, the weaver created the design of the weave. (See *Warp and Woof below*.)

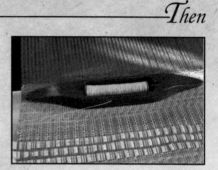

A shuttle with a bobbin of white thread.

An accomplished weaver could make the shuttle virtually fly back and forth across the loom. The work had a meditative quality as well:

> Lo! here 'twixt Heaven and Earth I swing,
> And whilst the Shuttle swiftly flies,
> With cheerful heart I work and sing
> And envy none beneath the skies.[13]

Now—

Shuttle generally refers to a vehicle that carries goods or people back and forth usually fairly short distances from one set place to another. Shuttle as a verb denotes the act of moving quickly back and forth from one location to another—just as the colonial shuttle hurried back and forth across the loom.

Spinster
—Then

The word **spinster** referred to a female who spun thread for sewing and weaving. The term might be used for a girl learning to perform the task so that upon marriage she could carry her skill into her own home, as well as for a woman who never married but who continued to help with the family spinning throughout the years. By 1806, Noah Webster's *A Compendious Dictionary of the English Language* indicated that the word referred also to a maiden woman.

Now

Spinster refers to an unmarried woman, usually one whose prospects for marriage, because of her age, appear slim. The word has a pejorative connotation, and its use today would be considered sexist.

Tenterhooks
Then

In colonial days, after woolen cloth was woven, it had to be cleaned of the lanolin oil and bits of dirt that might remain. The washed cloth then needed to be set out to dry in a manner that would prevent it from shrinking and wrinkling; so it was stretched onto a wooden tenter that had a close-set row of metal **tenterhooks** arranged along the sides of the frame, securely holding the cloth.

Tenterhooks on a beam in an old wool mill. Photograph courtesy of J. Edwards.

Now

To be on **tenterhooks** means to be anxious or emotionally strained by suspense. It takes no great stretch of the imagination to see the connection. As early as 1806 in his dictionary of words used in America, Noah Webster, defined tenter as "difficulty" or "trouble" as well as "a frame, an iron hook."[14]

Tow
Then

Tow was the mass of short golden-white flax fibers combed out from the long ones by heckling as part of the process of preparing the long fibers to be spun into linen thread to be woven into linen cloth. The short fiber tow was spun and then woven on a tow loom into rough burlap-type cloth or made into rope.

Now

The term **towhead** is derived from the resemblance of a child's hair color to that of the light tow. From the 1800s through today, towhead has meant a light-haired person. It is still used that way today.

Virgin
—Then

*V*irgin was one of a number words used by the colonists for a young unmarried girl. Such girls were also called "maidens" or "maids." A eulogy for a girl of just six began:

> *A Neighbors Tears dropt on ye grave of an Amiable Virgin, a*
> *pleasant Plant cut down in the blooming of her Spring vis; Mrs*
> *Rebecka Sewall Anno Aetatis 6, August ye 4th 1710.*[15]

Mrs was a shortened form of *Mistress* and was used for unmarried as well as married girls and women of a higher class. A mistress's husband and sons would be addressed as master while the husband and wife of a lower class were called goodman and goodwife.

Puritan society in early colonial days valued the sacrament of marriage and frowned upon bachelors and single women. If a still-unwed girl was no longer young, she was called an old maid; if she was particularly old—all of twenty-five—she might be called an ancient maid, and if older still—over thirty—a thornback. New Englanders, believing that being unmarried was a sign of God's ill favor, had a saying: "women dying maids lead apes in hell."[16]

In the early 1750s, one spurned lover taunted a woman named Rebecca Salisbury who rejected his proposal of marriage: "The proverb old—you know it well, that women dying maids, lead apes in hell." To which this lively, quick-witted young woman replied:

> *Lead apes in hell—tis no such thing;*
> *The story's told to fool us.*

> *But better there to hold a string,*
> *Than here let monkeys lead us.*[17]

Men, too, were encouraged to marry. The town of Eastham, Massachusetts, in 1695, issued this curious order:

> *Every unmarried man in the township shall kill six blackbirds or*
> *three crows while he remains single; as a penalty for not doing it,*
> *shall not be married until he obey this order.*[18]

Living alone was not tolerated in Massachusetts. In 1672, the county court of Essex, said that

> *being informed that John Littleale of Haverhill lay in a house by*
> *himself contrary to the law of the country, whereby he is subject*
> *to much sin and iniquity, which ordinarily are the companions*
> *and consequences of a solitary life, it was ordered ... he remove*
> *and settle himself in some orderly family in the town, and be*
> *subject to the orderly rules of family government.*[19]

Now

A **virgin** is a woman or man who has not yet had sexual intercourse.

Widow's peak
Then

A colonial **widow's peak** was a small cap with a pointed forepart or peak, which was worn by a widow to indicate her status. By the late 1700s, it was also used to refer to a person's hairline that formed a *V* at the center of the forehead. Superstition held that if a woman was born with a widow's peak, she would become a widow early in her married life.

Widows, also known as *relicts*, were numerous in colonial days, but they were also much in demand by men, especially widowers who were typically quick to remarry. With the mortality rate high from the harshness of life, the dangers of childbirth, and the prevalence of disease, it was not uncommon for a man or woman to be married several times. In 1777, while attending the Continental Congress, John Adams lodged in Philadelphia with a landlady *who has buried four Husbands, one Tailor, two shoemakers and Gilbert Tenant [Tennent], and still is ready for a fifth, and well deserves him too …[20]*

Many of our forefathers, including Benjamin Franklin, George Washington, Thomas Jefferson, and James Madison, were happily married for the first time to widows.

Now

A **widow's peak** refers to a person's hairline when it forms a distinct point at the upper center of the forehead.

Warp and Woof
Then

On colonial weaving looms, warp threads were laid lengthwise and the woof or weft–the cross threads–widthwise. The weaver interwove the woof threads into the warp threads. The weaver would work the treadles (the wooden levers) used to raise and lower selected warp threads creating openings, called sheds, through which to send the shuttle with its bobbin of weft (woof) thread back and forth. Each pass of the shuttle would go through a different set of sheds thus creating the pattern of the finished cloth.

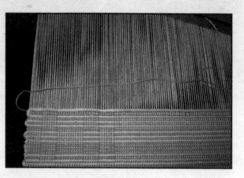

Warp and woof on loom at GBT.

Now

Warp and woof means, metaphorically, the entire intricate structure, texture, or fabric of something. One might talk of the warp and woof of early colonial life. Weavers also still use those terms for the threads on their loom just as the colonists did.

WOMEN AND WORK
Chapter Notes:

1   Ulrich, *Goodwives*, 77-78.

2   Nylander, 87.

3   Butterfield, ed., 127.

4   Fischer, *Albion's Seed*, 84.

5   Earle, *Colonial Dames*, 309.

6   Dow, 261-262.

7   Dow, 262.

8   *College Courant*, January 21, 1871. in De Vere, *Americanisms*, 268.

9   Earle, *Colonial Dames*, 244.

10 Butterfield, ed., 172.

11 Dow, 180.

12 Bassett, 32.

13 Earle, *Home Life*, 88.

14 Webster, 309.

15 Earle, *Colonial Dames*, 41.

16 Fischer, *Albion's Seed*, 77.

17 *Diary of Anna Green Winslow*, 120.

18 Earle, *Customs and Fashions*, 37.

19 Fischer, *Albion's Seed*, 73.

20 Butterfield, ed., 171.

HOME

If you traveled back in time and entered a colonial home of the 1600s and 1700s, you would look in vain for a bathroom, a toilet,

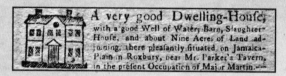

Dwelling house for sale, the Boston Evening Post, *November 15, 1773.*

a sink, a stove, a furnace, or even a box of matches. Yet, through the years, the colonists continually refined both the style and comfort of their homes far beyond what they had known when they first arrived on New England's shores. They painted the woodwork of their rooms in rich colors—among them greens, yellows, chocolate browns, and expensive Prussian blue. They had parlors in which to show off their best high-post beds (yes, their beds) complete with rugs to cover the beds and curtains hung to keep out the cold. They had cupboards filled with chinaware, stoneware, Delftware, pewter, and silver. They had table boards and tea boards to set on frames or trestles, as well as different forms of tables. They might have had looking glasses (mirrors), sconces, desks, chairs with cushions, books, and more.

In 1735, a notice for sale at "Publick Vendue" of the household contents of a wealthy merchant gives a picture of the furnishings his home contained:

Wallpapers offered for sale in the Boston Evening Post, *November 17, 1773.*

> Beds, Bedding, a Couch, Chairs, handsome Japan'd Tea Tables, Walnut and Mahogany Tables, Chest of Drawers, Peer Glasses, Sconces, Glass Arms, China Ware, Metzotinto and other Prints, several valuable large Pieces of Paintings, one handsome large Carpet 9 Foot 6 Inches by 6 Foot 6 Inches, a fashionable yellow

> *Camblet Bed lin'd with Satten, a great easy Chair and Window*
> *Curtains, suitable for a Room, a Field Bedstead and Bed, the*
> *covering a Blew Harrateen, Kitchen Furniture, as Pewter of the*
> *best sort, Copper, Brass and Iron, a parcel of Books and some*
> *Shop Goods[1]*

His was one of the few homes in the early 1700s to have a carpet laid upon the floor. Until the mid-1700s, carpets were used as covers for tables, and rugs as covers for beds.

By the late 1700s, even those of lesser means were furnishing their homes with what in prior years were considered luxury goods. The Marquis de Chastellux had come to America to serve with the French forces aiding General Washington and the colonial army during the Revolutionary War. He was a keen observer of American life, and the trend he saw troubled him:

> *Such is the general equality of condition that those things*
> *which everywhere else would be regarded as luxuries are here*
> *considered necessities. So it is that the salary of a workingman*
> *must not only provide subsistence for his family, but also*
> *comfortable furniture for the home, tea and coffee for his wife,*
> *and a silk dress to put on every time she goes out.[2]*

Yet, however finely furnished his home, no one, wealthy or poor, was exempt from the harshness inherent in life in those times. The weather, known as the Little Ice Age[3] by modern climatologists, was far colder than New England weather today. One writer noted:

> *The cold we have now seems to exceed all recollection or idea, as*
> *well as it does all endurance. I had almost spoiled my letter with*
> *a lump of black ice, which hung from my pen just now. [4]*

In the winter of 1780, it was so cold that even the wells froze, leaving this man to complain:

> *Our lowest and best well has been ever since ye great Storm,*
> *froze up and filled with Snow that we have not been able to use*
> *it, till today, when we got it open.[5]*

Though Abigail Adams, like all of her compatriots, had to suffer the winter cold that penetrated bedchambers sufficient to freeze water in wash bowls and ink in inkwells, she was fortunate to own a long-handled brass bed warmer that she could fill with coals and run between her sheets before she climbed into bed. But to keep her household running, fires lit, and food cooked, she had to have nearly fifty cords of wood cut and stacked, a job for which she was fortunate to have sons who helped. Much of home life revolved around the kitchen fireplace, and she had to guard against the ever-present danger of clothing catching fire as she cooked in the ashes and small fires on her hearth. She had to guard against the danger of being scalded when a large pot or iron kettle (some weighing up to forty pounds empty) fell from its hook or trammel as the long wooden lug pole holding it over the fire burned

Cooking on the hearth before the fireplace.

through. (Only when both the crane (the lug pole) and the trammels (the pot hangers) were made of iron did this danger cease to exist.) In addition, however refined her home, she, like all others, either used a chamber pot or trekked outside to the outhouse no matter the weather.

This was the life she and her compatriots lived, and they took pride and comfort in their homes, as we do today. John Greenleaf Whittier, born in Massachusetts in 1807, painted this bucolic picture as applicable to the 1700s as to the early 1800s:

> *Shut in from all the world without,*
> *We sat the clean-winged hearth about,*
> *Content to let the north-wind roar*
> *In baffled rage at pane and door,*
> *While the red logs before us beat*
> *The frost-line back with tropic heat; …*
>
> *The house dog on his paws outspread*
> *Laid to the fire his drowsy head,*
> *The cat's dark silhouette on the wall*
> *A couchant tiger's seemed to fall;*
> *And, for the winter fireside meet,*
> *Between the andirons' straddling feet,*

The mug of cider simmered slow,
The apples sputtered in a row,
And, close at hand, the basket stood
With nuts from brown October's woods.

What matter how the night behaved?
What matter how the north-wind raved?
Blow high, blow low, not all its snow
Could quench our hearth-fire's ruddy glow.[6]

Above the salt, below the salt

Then

Imported salt was a highly valued commodity in colonial times. In addition to being used to preserve meat, salt was sold in blocks from

TO BE SOLD,
On Board the Brigantine, BRISTOL, *John Skimmer*, Master,
The beſt of Lisbon SALT.
Enquire at *John Rowe's* Store, or on board the Brigantine, now lying at Rowe's Wharf.

An advertisement offering salt for sale, Boston Evening Post, *November 15, 1773.*

which pieces were chipped off, ground, usually in a large salt *mortar,* and put into some sort of dish for serving at the dining table. At first, the colonist used a single standing silver, glass, or fancy earthenware saltcellar—an imposing raised vessel that gave dignity to the dining table. The *salt* as it was called, was placed in such a position on the table that those seated **above the salt**, closer to the head of the household, were recognized as honored; those seated **below the salt,** were less esteemed. In the mid-1600s, Harvard College used its large silver saltcellar to separate the faculty and graduate students from the undergraduates when they sat together at table.

Salts were still being sold in 1773 as this advertisement in the *Boston Evening Post* shows:

> *Elizabeth Perkins has for Sale at her shop … a very large and*
> *Genteel Assortment of Cream colour'd Delph, Flint & Glass*
> *Ware, wholesale or retail, among which are cut, label'd, enamel'd,*
> *engrav'd & plain Quart, Pint, and ½ Pint Decanters, Cruets,*

Salts, Wine and Water Glasses, Tumblers, Jellies, syllabub
Glasses, Orange Glasses, Salvers, Sugar Dishes, Pattie, Sweetmeat
and Pickle Saucers, Royal Arch Mason Glasses, Salt Linings,
Water Glasses, Candle Sticks, etc.[7]

Salt has been a highly valued commodity throughout history. It is said that a Roman soldier was paid in salt; thus the expression to be "worth his salt."

Now

Above the salt is an expression signifying that the person so labeled is valued; **below the salt**, that he or she is less esteemed.

Backlog

Then

Three-footed skillet and pot.

The **backlog** was a large, thick, specially cut log, some five feet long. It rested in the ashes of the huge kitchen fireplace, burning comfortingly on cold days while the housewife assembled smaller, more controllable beds of hot coals of oak, chestnut, or hemlock at the front of the hearth. Over these small fires she placed her pipkins (earthenware pans or pots), and her cast iron posnets (pots with three feet), skillets, creepers and spiders (fry pans with three feet), gridirons (grill pans with three feet), and Dutch ovens (bake ovens). The backlog would burn slowly, often until the following morning, so that the housewife could enjoy its heat in the cold dawn when she came to start her morning cooking fires from the backlog's embers.

In a moment of nostalgia, one man wrote:

We children missed the bright fire light in the evenings. With the
big back log and fore stick and pine knots between, it made our

great kitchen look very bright and cheerful … . And we used to love to sit around on the hearth and tell stories or listen to some older person telling a story. And when company would come in, they would all take turns in singing a song or telling a story.[8]

Now

A **backlog** now refers to a reserve from which goods or services can be drawn, a surplus, or a burdensome oversupply; alternatively, it is a body of work yet to be done or orders yet to be filled.

Board

Then

The **board,** used in the early days, was a large, flat, rectangular piece of wood, frequently hung on the wall until called into use. Then it was set upon trestles to make a table for a meal. In the seventeenth century when a family prepared for a more formal meal, they were said to have "laid the board." Sarah Knight, on her stay at a tavern in 1704, described:

> *Here, having called for something to eat, y* woman bro't a Twisted thing like a cable, but something whiter; and laying it on the bord, tugg'd for life to bring it into a capacity to spread; w[ch] having wth great pains accomplished, she serv'd in a dish of Pork and Cabage, I suppose the remains of dinner.*[9]

Legend has it that some boards had carved depressions in them so that food could be placed directly upon the board in front of each diner without the need for trenchers (rectangular wooden plates shared by two people), chargers (pewter plates) or, for that matter, board cloths. (Board cloths, now called tablecloths, are frequently found listed in early inventories.) When the meal was completed, the board would be washed down and hung again on its peg.

Board was also the word for a table that had been set with the utensils for a meal. Interestingly, forks did not appear in colonial inventories until the early 1700s. Before that, people used the pointed end of knives or used spoons or their fingers to bring food to their mouths.

Board also stood for meals themselves. Abigail Adams wrote to her husband, John:

The extravagance of Board is greater there than here tho here everything is at such prices as was not ever before known.[10]

The expression **above board**, in use from the early 1600s, meant open, straightforward, and in sight of all those assembled at the board. In a game of cards, if a player's hands were above board, it was thought he could not be cheating.

Now

Board refers to a piece of stiff cardstock used for games or a rectangular piece of flat, sawn wood. In the phrase *room and board*, still retaining the meaning of the old usage, board refers to meals. **Above board** retains its metaphorical meaning of open, in plain sight, without trickery.

Chaffing dish
Then

A **chaffing dish** was a utilitarian wire or earthenware basket into which hot coals were placed to create a brazier or warming device. One early child-rearing book suggested warming the baby's diapers (then called clouts): "Have ever ready a chaffen-dish with fire … to warm clouts."[11]

Now

A **chafing dish** (with the second *f* dropped) consists of a stand on which a cooking pan may be placed over a heat source—a candle or a water bath—such that the food in the pan is heated gently. The chafing dish is often an attractive serving piece that is brought to table to serve guests.

Chairman of the board
Then

*A*t mealtime, the family would gather around the set table. If the family was fortunate enough to own a good armchair, perhaps a high-standing, carved oak one with a leather seat, that chair would be given to the father or honored guest, and the rest of the family would sit on smaller benches, forms, or stools. In early colonial days, chairs were scarce and were thought to carry with them a connotation of authority. Thus the father or honored guest was the first **chairman of the board**.

Now

Chairman of the board is the person who presides over a company's corporate meetings and oversees the company's decisions and policies. He or she holds the leadership role on the board of directors. This meaning likely derived from the chairman's being considered the honored person at the table, as he was in colonial days.

Chowder

Then

The word **chowder** was the colonists' word for the Breton fishermen's fish stew. The French fishermen would *faire la chaudière*, that is, set up a big pot or cauldron called a *chaudière* into which fellow fishermen would throw a mess of their fresh-caught fish, some biscuit, and savory seasonings. These ingredients would be cooked into a stew, with a share of the tasty dish given to each who contributed to the pot that day. Anglicizing the French word, the early New England colonists used the word *chowder* to describe this stew they commonly cooked in the pot. Inventive colonial housewives modified the recipe, adding bacon and onion in addition to the biscuit and later, potatoes, and cooking it, sometimes in cider and champagne.

Now

Chowder refers to a delicious thick stew-like soup made from fish, clams, or corn, together with salt pork and vegetables all usually cooked in a milk or tomato base. However benign "milk or tomato base" may sound, within the phrase lies a bitter rivalry between New Englanders who believe that only a thick, rich chowder made with potatoes and milk is real chowder and New Yorkers who believe that only the thinned reddish soup made with tomatoes is the real chowder. In fact, Maine passed a law in the 1930s prohibiting the addition of tomatoes to New England clam chowder. Many still think Maine was right to do so.

Corn

————————————————————————————————————*Then*

The English settlers used the word **corn** as it was used in England, to mean all cereals—rye,

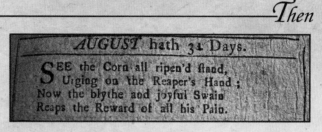

AUGUST hath 31 Days.

SEE the Corn all ripen'd ftand,
Urging on the Reaper's Hand;
Now the blythe and joyful Swain
Reaps the Reward of all his Pain.

From The Connecticut Almanack *1773.*

wheat, oats, and barley. So when the Indians introduced their native corn, the colonists needed to give it a name. To distinguish this new plant, they called it Indian corn. (In Britain it was called *maize*.) It was the Indians who taught the colonists how to fertilize (placing a dead fish on top of each kernel of corn), tend, harvest, and even grind and cook the corn. The meal ground from Indian corn was called Indian meal or sometimes just *injun* or *Indian*. Thus, Indian pudding was a pudding made with Indian cornmeal, not a pudding made by Indians. *Rye n' injun* was coarse bread made from cornmeal, rye flour, yeast, and molasses.

Parched corn was what we now call popcorn. Governor John Winthrop wondered at the miracle of the popped kernel that turned inside out, revealing itself "white and floury within."[12]

According to a 1623 Massachusetts ordinance, corn and beans were to be the tokens used in voting. A corn kernel signified a vote for the candidate and a bean signified a vote against. To ensure there was no voter fraud, the regulation stipulated:

> *If any free-man shall put in more than one Indian corn or bean*
> *he shall forfeit for every such offence Ten Pounds.*[13]

Now————————————————————————————————

Corn refers to the golden, white, or even purple, blue, or red kernels that grow on cobs. It is widely planted throughout the United States and is used today not only for eating and baking, but for use in everything from antibiotics to food, from drink sweeteners to livestock feed, from cornstarch to the fuel additive ethanol.

Dairy

Then

Butter churn.

The **dairy**, sometimes called the *buttery* or cheese room, was the room in more affluent colonial homes where the milk from the family's cows and goats would be brought to be processed into butter and cheese, work done by women in colonial days. A house offered for sale in the *Boston Gazette* in 1761 was described as having two dairies:

> The Mansion House has 4 Rooms on the lower Floor, besides a Dairy Room, 11 good Chambers on the two upper Floors ... . A deep Cellar runs under the whole House, the walls of which are laid in Lime Mortar, with three good Arches, one large enough for a Winter Dairy Room.[14]

Cows. *Detail from an Enoch Wood Staffordshire platter c. 1800. From a private collection.*

Since there was no refrigeration, families needed to transform the milk into forms that would both nourish and last. Cheese was an important source of protein in the colonial diet. Whether a woman had a dairy or not, she would likely have equipment for making cheese and butter. When Mary Lane and her sisters were married in the late 1700s, they were each given a "cow, wooden milk pails, and a churn" as part of their marriage portion (today called a dowry).[15] From the first days of settlement, cows and goats were highly valued for their milk; and cows, in particular, for their labor, beef, hides, tallow, horn, and their dung for fertilizer.

Now

In due course, production of dairy products ceased being a domestic enterprise and became a commercial one. Accordingly, you can see how, as a result of this commercialization, the meaning changed. A **dairy** became a business operation that processes and/or sells milk and milk products such as butter, cream, cheeses, cottage cheese, and sour cream. Happily, a growing number of people are reviving the practice of making cheese at home. These artisanal cheeses are gaining in both quality and popularity.

Done to a turn

Roasting oven showing holes for rotation of spit.

Meat and poultry were roasted in front of the kitchen fire, at times in a metal reflector oven that had a spit to hold the meat. On some of these colonial roasting ovens, the handle of the spit had a small attached arm that was inserted into a set of holes surrounding the spit handle on the side of the oven. At timed intervals, the cook, a servant, or one of the children would move the arm around one additional hole until the spitted meat had been turned all the way around, and the meat was said to be **done to a turn**.

Wealthy families could afford a clockwork jack and spit that turned the meat by means of gears and belts, a clock mechanism, and a slowly dropping weight. When the mechanism was wound, it set the spit in motion for a given length of time. This constant turning provided more even cooking and ensured that the meat was done to a turn.

Clockwork jack mechanism to turn meat on a spit in front of fire.

The early settlers and those who later could not afford the special pans and jacks might fix a strong string to a peg in the ceiling and hang the haunch of meat or the bird in front of the fireplace. The string was wound tight and allowed to unwind and rewind from the momentum until the meat was done to a turn. Legend has it that the French cook who accompanied Baron von Steuben to Valley Forge during the Revolutionary War quit in disgust saying that since any common wagoner could cook meat by hanging it on a string, his skills were no longer needed.[16]

Dutch oven
Then

*T*he **Dutch oven** (called Dutch because the Netherlanders originally made the best of these large cast iron pots) was the first colonial bake oven. Cooks who did not have a beehive-baking oven built into their fireplaces used a Dutch oven to bake breads and puddings. The pot had a tight-fitting rimmed lid, either flat or curved into a depression in the center, onto which burning coals were placed. The pot would then be placed over a low fire on the hearth, thus making an efficient oven in which to bake food.

Now

Today's **Dutch oven** is a large enamel, cast iron, or other metal pan with a high domed, tight-fitting lid, frequently used to cook beef pot roasts or fowl.

Easy chair
Then

*I*ntroduced in New England in colonial days, the **easy chair** or great chair was built with a deep comfortable down-filled cushion and high winged sides. It was the first chair to be fully upholstered—seat, back, and arms. Some had a wooden substructure into which a chamber pot could be fitted, to be used when the upholstered seat cushion was lifted. (The deep apron of the chair hid the pot from view.) Kept in the bedchamber, the easy chair was primarily used by the elderly and the infirm or by those tending to the needs of the infirm. For one man, years had gone by since he was "capable of sleeping in a bed by reason of his decrepit condition, by the rheumatism, he has always slept in his great chair."[17]

Sometimes a young person as well might enjoy the comforts of the easy chair. Recuperating from a cold one particularly frigid day, twelve-year old Anna Winslow wrote of the weather:

*I know nothing about it but hearsay for I am in aunt's chamber …
with a nice fire … sitting in Aunt's easy chair, with a tall three
leav'd screen at my back, & I am very comfortable.[18]*

Now

An **easy chair** is a large comfortable chair usually found in the family room,
living room, or den. (It is no longer outfitted with a chamber pot, we trust.)

Hall
Then

*I*n first-settlement colonial homes in New England, the **hall** was the
name given to the main room, frequently the only room except perhaps
for a loft or chamber above. The hall, sometimes called the keeping room,

*The formal 1768 entryway of the Golden Ball
Tavern.*

served multiple functions. Here the
family gathered to cook, eat, spin,
work, sing, read the Bible, converse
around the fire, and sleep. In time,
houses were enlarged first with a
parlor built to share the central
chimney with the hall, and then with
additional rooms—back parlors,
separate kitchens, and chambers
(upstairs bedrooms). Some colonists
added on a lean-to—a structure with
a steep roofline added to the back of
the original house to accommodate a
separate kitchen.

By 1767, New Englanders'
expectations of a sufficient dwelling
place had advanced far beyond the
simple hall. John Adams remarked
on a home he had visited that still
offered but a single room for the
family:

> *One Chamber, which serves them for Kitchen, Cellar,*
> *dining Room, Parlour, and Bed Chamber .... There are the*
> *Conveniences and ornaments of a Life of Poverty. These the*
> *comforts of the poor ... This is Want.*[19]

As homes became more substantial and refined, many were built with wide central passageways, though these were still usually not designated as halls. A visiting Englishwoman in the 1760s described one this way:

> *Through the middle of the house was a very wide passage, with*
> *opposite front and back doors, which in summer admitted a*
> *stream of air peculiarly grateful to the languid senses. It was*
> *furnished with chairs and pictures like a summer parlour.*
> *Here the family usually sat in hot weather, when there were no*
> *ceremonious strangers.*[20]

Colonists called the entry space or center hallway in the 1700s Georgian home an entry, entryway, or great entry (to distinguish it from a smaller side entry.)

Now

A **hall** is the entry room or a passageway running from front to back through a house or building. It can also refer to a main large meeting or function room in a nonresidential building, and that usage, at least, retains a bit of the colonial connection.

Housewarming gift
Then

The colonial **housewarming gift** was aptly named, for it was a gift of burning coals or wood that the gift giver brought from her established home fire and gave to the newly arrived family to use for lighting the fire in the kitchen fireplace. Once her kitchen fire was established, the prudent housewife would bank it each night, carefully raking ashes over the live coals that could then be used to start a fire during the night if someone became ill or the next morning to prepare breakfast. Much of a woman's life revolved around the kitchen fire (cooking, baking, washing, ironing, rendering fat, and soap and candle making), and if she carelessly allowed her fire to go out, she had either to relight it with a flint and steel or go begging to her neighbors for a lighted coal. Friction matches were not commonly available until the 1830s.

Now

A **housewarming gift** is any gift given to welcome people newly moved into their home. A housewarming party is one given to celebrate taking possession of a home.

Humble pie
Then

*T*he **humbles,** to the colonists, were the entrails, liver, heart, and other inner parts of a deer. One recipe in the 1600s instructed, "take ye humbles of a deer."[21] Some say that when the animal was slaughtered, the honored guests and important family members ate the venison while the servants and lesser folk ate the humbles minced and baked into **humble pie**.

Now

To eat **humble pie** means to apologize, to admit error, to reduce one's self to acknowledged subordination by reason of prior conduct or assertion demonstrated to be wrong. This is not a light "sorry," but rather an expression of regret and apology.

Glazed earthenware chamber pot (5 ½" high by 8 ½" wide).

John
Then

*J*ohn, also called Cousin John or Cousin Jake, was a name for the portable ceramic chamber pot kept near the bed and used as a toilet at night by those who could afford such a luxury. Freshmen at Harvard in the early 1700s were prohibited from using each other's "cuz John."[22] A century earlier in England, chamber pots were known as *jakes*.

Now

John is slang for toilet. Toilets as we know them today did not exist nor were they given the name of *toilet* until the 1820s when cities (Philadelphia first in 1820 and Boston in 1823) installed sewers and waterworks into which waste water could flow.

Powder room

Then

A **powder room** was the room in which colonists had their hair or wigs powdered. Through much of the 1700s, most men and women wore wigs that were carefully set and, starting around 1710, powdered. Since powdering was a messy job done at the last minute when the wig was on the wearer's head, the person having his or her wig powdered would cover his shoulders with a sheet and hold a paper cone over his face to keep from choking. Having a separate powder room was a luxury. Implements such as powdering puffs and bags as well as powdering machines and a whole variety of powders, plain and scented, brown to blue, were sold. In 1732, the Boston grocer, John Merrett, offered "Hair-Powder, powder Blue."[23] And in 1772, the jewelers Roberts and Lee, "Opposite the Old Brick Meeting-house, Cornhill, Boston," offered for sale "hair powder scented & plain, powder knives, dressing and tail combs, tortoise shell pole combs, black hair pins." [24]

Women who did not own wigs could mold their own hair into ornate, high piles, held in place with grease, with the whole construction powdered. Some women wore rolls that they placed under their natural hair to give it height and volume. In 1771 young Anna Winslow described her new roll to her mother:

> *I had my Heddus roll on. Aunt Storer said
> it ought to be made less, Aunt Deming said*

Two-hole outhouse.

it ought not to be made at all. It makes my head ach (sic) and
burn and itch like anything Mama. This famous Roll is not made
wholly of a Red-Cow Tail but is a mixture of that & horsehair
very coarse & a little human hair of a yellow hue that I suppose
was taken out of the back part of an old wig.[25]

These rolls could be made to any height and weight a woman wished. As one poet lampooned:

Give Chloe a bushel of horsehair and wool,
Of paste and pomatum a pound,
Ten yards of gay ribbon to deck her sweet skull
And gauze to encompass it round.[26]

When a woman undid this concoction in the privacy of her home, she was said to have "let her hair down."

Now

A **powder room** is another name for a small bathroom. In addition to its primary use, women retire to the powder room to tend to their makeup and hair. The term *powder room* was never used as a name for the outhouse, though other euphemisms such as *necessary house*, the *necessary*, or the *house of office* were used. Bathrooms in the modern sense did not come into being until the 1840s, and then they were "bathing" rooms with a tub, available hot water, and a means of draining the tub to the outdoors.

Sauce

Then

Sauce or **sass** referred to all vegetables, cooked or raw. In the fall of 1744, having gathered in his crop, farmer Abner Sanger wrote that he had prepared "a place in the cellar to put sauce in to keep it from freezing."[27] The vegetables common to the colonial garden were beans, peas, carrots, potatoes, cabbage, parsnips, onions, pumpkins, turnips, and green squash. Parsnips, carrots, and the like were designated *long sass*, while onions, turnips, potatoes, and such were called *short sass*.

Colonial housewives frequently stewed or potted their salted (preserved) meat with green and root vegetables; this slow cooking made the meat tender, seasoned the stew with the salt from the meat, and turned the vegetables into what was called "green sauce."

Sass in the sense of *sauce* was also used for applesauce or other stewed fruit. Cranberries, sometimes called bearberries because the bears so loved them, were early on boiled with sugar to make cranberry sauce, and pumpkins similarly to make pumpkin sauce. Madam Sarah Knight, whose journal of her travels between Boston and New York in 1704 has provided generations with a firsthand account of life on the road, wrote of one stop:

> And that night Lodgd at Stonington and had Rost Beef and
> pumpkin sause for supper.[28]

So common were pumpkins that a ninety-six-year-old woman wrote in 1785:

> If fresh meat be wanting to fill up our dish,
> We have carrots and turnips as much as we wish;
> And is there a mind for a delicate dish
> We repair to the clam banks, and there we catch fish.
> Instead of pottage and puddings and custards and pies,
> Our pumpkins and parsnips are common supplies;
> We have pumpkins at morning and pumpkins at noon;
> If it was not for pumpkins we should be undone.[29]

The word *sauce* came early on to mean impertinence as well. From the accompanying newspaper article, it appears that the youth in the late 1700s were thought to be growing increasingly saucy and unacceptably impertinent as evidenced by their use of profanity.

Messi'rs. PRINTERS,
If you suppose the following Hints and Queries will have any tendency towards a reformation, be pleased to publish them in your useful paper.

THERE was a time when it was a very rare thing to hear a prophane oath uttered in the street, but now the very children are permitted to use such language that one can scarcely pass a rod without hearing of many; and what appears truly alarming is, that heads of families, and persons who we have a right to expect better of, pass by in the hearing without noticing them.

From the Boston Gazette and Country Journal, *August 26, 1782.*

Now

Now——————————————————————————

Sauce is a relish or dressing served to enhance the flavor of food. The word also still means impertinent, as in *saucy*.

Set the table
——————————————————————————*Then*

To the first colonists, to **set the table** meant to place a wooden board that served as a dining table onto a pair of trestles (today's sawhorses). Until the latter part of the 1700s, there were no designated dining rooms. In this nineteenth century recounting of the cherished family memory of President George Washington's visit to the Monroe Tavern in Lexington, Massachusetts, in 1789, daughter Sarah says:

> *Our loved President has journied here to Lex. & has took dinner at our very House ... . There stood my Father and step-mother at the tap-room Door ... . My Father looked grandly in his rejimentels and proud indeed was I of him as he led the way to the Dinner-room prepar'd for Mr. Washington in the upper room.*[30]

The table could be set in the warmest room in winter and the coolest in summer.

Now——————————————————————————

To **set the table** means to put plates, glasses, silverware, and the like on the table in preparation for a meal.

Sleep tight
——————————————————————————*Then*

The first documented use of the phrase **sleep tight** did not appear until the mid-1800s. Yet, knowing what we do of colonial beds, it is no wonder that people attribute the expression to the colonists. Colonists often slept on beds (meaning mattresses) that rested on bedsteads (frames) strung with a lattice of ropes. Dowries show "bedsteads and cords" being given to

Folding rope-strung bed with bed key to tighten ropes.

daughters upon their marriages. The bed ropes or cords would stretch with use, lose their tension, and sag. If someone used the wooden rope key to pull the slack ropes tighter for better support of the mattress, the slumberer might well be said to **sleep tight.** The rest of the expression, "Don't let the bedbugs bite," had it been used, would have been an equally sincere wish, for in the days when beds (mattresses) were filled with straw, corn husks, or feathers, even the most conscientious housekeeper might be unable to prevent an infestation of bedbugs. And since most people slept more than one to a bed, sometimes many more than one, and since personal hygiene in colonial days was episodic at best, bedbugs were a common nuisance. One traveler staying in a tavern in July 1778 noted in his diary:

> *The Beds were filled with Bugs, which fell upon me with such fury as to drive me from my bed.*[31]

And on that same trip, at another tavern:

> *Beds were good, the linen clean, but the bedsteads were infested with Bugs; and I laid on the floor.* [32]

Goose down provided the best filling for beds, but not until the late 1700s was a housewife able purchase sufficient quantities of such down from a vendor. Instead, if she was fortunate, as were many brides, she might be given the feathers as part of her dowry. If not, she likely had to pluck the forty or fifty pounds of feathers from her own geese or collect them over months from her neighbors. One man recalled:

> *Every decent family had its flock of geese, of course, which was picked thrice a year, despite the noisy remonstrances of both goose and gander.*[33]

A humorous anecdote sheds light on the complications of keeping geese to feather a bed:

> *My grandparents' geese were in the cellar where the wine was*
> *kept. The faucet on one of the wine kegs was open and the geese*
> *drank the wine. They got drunk, keeled over, and passed out!*
> *When my grandparents found the geese in the cellar, passed*
> *out, they thought they had died of something. They couldn't eat*
> *them because they might have died of something awful, so they*
> *plucked them all to use the feathers for feather beds. And then*
> *the geese woke up. They woke up and made a whole lot of noise.*
> *My grandparents had kept them tied on a string to the house*
> *for the rest of the summer until their feathers grew back so they*
> *wouldn't wander too far and get cold.*[34]

An interesting note: Parents slept mainly downstairs, their best bed complete with woven bed curtains, bed rugs, quilts, and covers being located in the best parlor or hall, while children slept mainly upstairs.

Now

Sleep tight is an expression used to wish someone a restful night's sleep.

Stove

Then

A **stove** in colonial days was another name for a pot with a tight-fitting lid used to cook a piece of game or meat. Women cooked in front of the large open fireplace in the kitchen either by hanging pots and kettles from a wooden or iron crane on trammels or pothooks directly over the main fire, or by placing fry pans, gridirons, Dutch ovens, and such over smaller beds of coals they prepared on the hearth. Stoves used for heating bedchambers and parlors only slowly found their way into colonial homes in the later part of the 1700s.

Now

A **stove** is an apparatus that generates heat to cook food or to warm a room on a chilly day. Cook stoves appeared in the early 1800s but only slowly gained in popularity in the 1830s and beyond. One woman reminisced:

> *How well do I remember that Wilson-Benton stove*
> *That father bought and paid for in cloth us girls had wove*
> *The people how they wondered when we got the thing to go*
> *They swore 'twould burst and kill us all some fifty years ago.* [35]

Even though the waist-high cooking surfaces freed women from kneeling down to cook among the coals and ashes on the hearth, many housewives resisted the newfangled inventions that required them to learn entirely new cooking techniques. One inventive salesman tried poetry to interest folks in the stove in 1837:

> *Now ladies all and gentlemen.*
> *We pray you give attention,*
> *Whilst we relate a real tale*
> *About a new invention.*
>
> *One Johnny Moore of Yankee blood,*
> *A cute and cunning fellow,*
> *He made himself a Cooking Stove*
> *By gosh! It was a whaler.*
>
> *Four holes upon its top it had,*
> *And rims both big and little,*
> *So he could boil his dinner in*
> *Most any kind of kettle.*
>
> *A darn'd great oven, too, it had,*
> *As big as Granny's apron,*
> *In which he always baked his bread,*
> *While Molly fried the bacon … .*
>
> *It took but mighty little fire*
> *To cook a rousing dinner;*
> *'Twould bake his bread and boil his pot,*
> *And warm a chilly sinner … .* [36]

Tin stove used to heat bed chamber.

Sugarloaf

—Then

$\mathcal{R}$efined sugar, a true luxury in colonial days, came from the West Indies in the form of the large, nine- to ten-pound cone-shaped **sugarloaf**, wrapped in a distinctive blue paper. Small pieces of the hard sugar would be snipped off the loaf with special sugar shears, nippers or cutters, sometimes called sugar devils, and used in lump form or ground fine with a mortar and pestle. John Merrett, an ingenious grocer even named his establishment the Three Sugar Loaves and Cannister. In 1732 he sold, in addition to other foodstuffs:

> *Cocoa, Chocolate, Tea, Bohea and Green, Coffee raw and roasted,*
> *all sorts of loaf, powder and Muscovado Sugar, Sugar-Candy brown*
> *and white, candy'd Citron, ...*[37]

Abigail Adams wrote to her husband, John, about the prices of goods in Boston in August 1776 during the war:

> *As to provisions there is no Scarcity. Tis true they are high ...*
> *Our New England Rum is 4 Shillings pr. Gallon, Molasses*
> *the same price. Loaf Sugar 2s. 4d. pr. pound ... . In short one*
> *hundred pound two year ago would purchase more than two will*
> *now.*[38]

If refined sugar was too expensive, molasses would serve. According to the observant British soldier Thomas Anburey, detained in Cambridge in 1777:

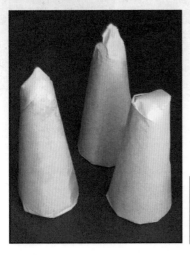

> *The gentry of both sexes*
> *are hospitable and good-*
> *natured, with an air of*
> *civility in their behavior ...*
> *both sexes have universally,*
> *and even proverbially, bad*
> *teeth, which must probably*
> *be occasioned by their eating*

Sugarloaves.

Sugar nippers.

so much molasses, making use of it at all meals, and even eating it with greasy pork. [39]

Now

Sugarloaf is the name given to objects that resemble large cone-shaped loaves of sugar. Mountains in the United States bear the name Sugarloaf from this resemblance. Sugar in loaf form is still in common use on the African continent today.

Warming pan

Then

The colonial **warming pan** was a long-handled, covered metal pan into which hot coals were placed. The hot pan was then inserted between the sheets of a bed and moved quickly around so that the chill was taken off. Lucky was the person who, on a cold winter's night, hopped into such a warmed bed, for he or she would not have to suffer the icy shock of freezing cold sheets. With no fire at all in the bedchambers, or a small one at best, the winter cold penetrated rooms enough to freeze water in wash bowls and ink in inkwells. On September 16, 1774, Abigail Adams wrote to her husband, John, then in Philadelphia for the first Continental Congress:

> *How warm your climate may be I know not, but I have had my bed warmed these two nights.* [40]

Others who did not have warming pans resorted to wrapping hot bricks or stones in blanketing to warm their beds, while the more stoic New Englanders considered the shock of the cold bed to be character building.

On a comical note, Alexander Hamilton, attending a dinner in New York one evening in 1744, was surprised to hear his hostess call for a warming pan:

Warming pan.

I could not guess what she intended to do with it unless it was to warm her bed to go to sleep after dinner, but I found that it was used by way of a chaffing dish to warm our dish of clams.[41]

Foot stove.

Foot stoves were also in common use, though probably not to warm clams. They were small and boxed shaped, with pierced metal sides encased in a wooden frame with a handle for ease of carriage. Hot coals would be put into the foot stove to warm the feet of a traveler or a worshiper who had to spend a frigid winter's Sunday in an unheated meetinghouse. In January 1771, Old South recorded:

Whereas, danger is apprehended from the stoves that are frequently left in the meeting-house after the publick worship is over; Voted that the Saxton make diligent search on the Lords Day evening and in the evening after a Lecture, to see if any stoves are left in the house, and that if he find any there he take them to his house; and it is expected that the owners of such stoves make reasonable satisfaction to the Saxton for his trouble before they take them away.[42]

Lacking such a stove, worshipers sometimes took hot potatoes or even their dogs to the meetinghouse to provide warmth.

Now

A **warming pan** is a decorative long-handled metal pan evocative of an earlier day when such devices were both a luxury and a necessity.

HOME

Chapter notes:

1 Dow, 110.

2 Garrett, 254.

3 Fischer, *Albion's Seed*, 52.

4 Garrett, 183.

5 Nylander, 79.

6 Earle, *Home Life*, 29-30.

7 Dexter, 28.

8 Nylander, 102.

9 Knight, 4-5.

10 Butterfield, ed., 171.

11 Lederer, 46.

12 Earle, *Customs and Fashions,* 148-149.

13 Earle, *Home Life,* 56.

14 Dow, 218.

15 Nylander, 62.

16 Story from Whitehill, 10.

17 Nylander, 37.

18 Garrett, 190.

19 Wolf, 59.

20 Cummings, xxii.

21 Lederer, 117.

22 Flexner, 18-19. Despite the pervasive myth, Thomas Crapper did not invent the flushing toilet.

23 Dow, *Arts and Crafts,* 293.

24 Dow, *Arts and Crafts,* 71.

25 Earle, *Customs and Fashions,* 293.

26 Earle, *Customs and Fashions,* 295.

27 Nylander, 207.

28 Knight, 38.

29 Carlo, *Trammels,* 73.

30 Forbes and Eastman, *Taverns and Stagecoaches,* vol. II, 74-76.

31 Ellery, 478.

32 Ellery, 481.

33 Garrett, 110.

34 Garrett, 110.

35 Armentrout, 79.

36 Nylander, 215-216.

37 Dow, *Arts and Crafts,* 292-293. Muscovado sugar was a coarse brown sugar tasting strongly of molasses.

38 Butterfield, ed., 158-159.

39 Anburey, *Travels,* vol. 2, 68-69.

40 Butterfield, ed., 74.

41 Garrett, 81-82.

42 *Diary of Anna Green Winslow,* 113.

CLOTHING AND MATERIAL

*W*omen and men cared about their clothing in colonial days just as we do today; and they often strained against the restrictive Puritan sumptuary (clothing) laws that sought to impose modesty and simplicity of dress, prohibiting the making, selling, or wearing, except by gentlemen and gentlewomen, of clothing decorated with lace, brocade trim, silver or gold buttons. By law, people were expected to dress according to their rank. As they emerged from the poverty of their first settlement years, and as more and more non-Puritan settlers came to live in New England, those who could afford it put aside the coarse cloth and bought velvets, satins, silks, rich brocades, embroideries, hats, wigs (worn universally by the early 1700s), face powders, perfumes, ribbons, and gold and silver buttons and shoe buckles. While they still dressed more modestly than their English and European counterparts, they came to value gentility and refinement rather more than piety. These changes, as can be expected, did not come wholly without disapproval.

Mercy Warren, a colonial political commentator, sheds light on what women wore in the 1770s in this satirical poem. If asked to give up imported cloth for homespun she wrote, the women might be moved to ask:

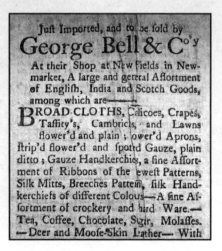

Imported goods advertised for sale in the New Hampshire Gazette and Historical Chronicle, *June 11, 1773.*

> *With lawns and lutestrings, blond and mecklin laces,*
> *Fringes and jewels, fans and tweezer cases,*
> *Gay cloaks and hats of every shape and size,*

Scarfs, cardinals and
ribbons of all dyes.
With ruffles stamped,
and aprons of tambour,
Tippets and
handkerchiefs at least
three score;
With finest muslins that
far India boasts, ...
Who'll wear the home-
spun produce of the
vales? ...
Add feathers, furs, rich
satins and ducapes
And head dresses in pyramidal shapes, ...
For when our manners are well understood
What in the scale is stomacher or hood? ...
This sweet temptation could not be withstood,
Though for her purchase paid her father's blood.[1]

To the Ladies who affect showing their White
Stockings, *excerpted from an article printed in the*
Boston Gazette and Country Journal, *August 26, 1782.*

To learn of the latest London fashions, the cut, stitching, and decoration,
women might purchase or pay to see a fashion doll, called a Baby, one of
which was advertised in July 1733 in *The New England Weekly Journal*:

To be seen at Mrs. Hannah Teatts Mantua Maker at the Head
of Summer Street Boston a Baby drest after the Newest Fashion
of Mantues and Night Gowns & everything belonging to a dress.
Latilly arrived on Capt. White from London, any Ladies that
desire to see it may either come or send, she will be ready to wait
on 'em, if they come to the House it is Five Shilling & if she waits
on 'em it is Seven Shilling.[2]

Bib and tucker
—Then

Colonial women sometimes wore a **bib** as an attached upper part of their
decorative aprons. In addition, women tucked or stitched linen or lace
ruffles, called **tuckers,** into the necklines of their gowns. In Anna Winslow's

1770 diary, she described her dress for a party (attended only by girls, so there was "no rudeness I can assure you") at her finishing school in Boston:

> *I was dressed in my yelloe coat, black bib and apron, black feathers on my head, my paste comb and all my paste garnet marquasett & jet pins, together with my silver plume—my locket, rings, black collar round my neck, black mitts and yards of blue ribbon (black and blue in high tast) striped tucker & ruffles (not my best) and my silk shoes completed my dress.*[3]

Now

Best bib and tucker means one's best clothing. To have on your best bib and tucker is to be all dressed up.

Diaper
—Then

*I*n colonial days, **diaper** was a type of cloth, usually linen, that was woven with a small but decorative diamond-weave or flower pattern, frequently used for making napkins and table covers. The *Boston News-Letter* in May 1738 advertised:

> *Wig Ribbons, Cauls, Raw and Ballandine Silk, fine Needles, Holland, Diaper and other Tapes and Sundry other Things in Millanary and Haberdashery Ware. Likewise, Grograms, Tiffenies, Lutestring and Alamode, Damask and Diaper Table Cloths …*[4]

The diapers used on a baby's bottom in colonial days were called clouts. They were often made from the material called diaper, which must have had good absorbency. An advertisement in the *Boston News-Letter* December 18, 1760, offered for sale "clouting diaper."[5]

Colonial-era paintings of young girls as well as boys below the age of six or so hide the clouts, showing the children always in long frocks. Such gowns made good sense for girls

Primitive portrait of William Pitt Jones, age six.

and especially for boys, until they were out of clouts and could be breeched and could handle the buttons of their breeches (pants) on their own. The frocks or gowns could readily be altered to fit the growing child and then re-altered to be passed on to the next baby.

Now—————————————————————

The word **diaper** refers to the rectangles of cotton material covering babies' bottoms and fastened with safety pins or tapes at the waist. Cloth diapers have now been almost entirely replaced by disposable paper "diapers."

Frock
—————————————————————*Then*

A **frock** was a long, loose over-garment that slipped over the wearer's head. Frocks were worn by adults as well as children to keep the clothes underneath clean. Men farming or doing outdoor labor would wear woolen frocks in winter and lighter cotton or linen frocks in summer.

In a 1731 notice for a runaway, the master, whose apprentice had fled, wrote that he had recently been seen "with a frock & trouzers on." [6]

And in 1751, at the launch of the brig Halifax, the *Boston Gazette* noted:

> *The Carpenters that built her were dress'd in clean white Frocks and Trowsers, Clean ruffle Shirts, and Gold-laced Hats.*[7]

Fringed shirts, worn by the Continental Army as part of the uniform with linen overalls, were also called frocks.

Now—————————————————————

A girl's or young woman's dress is called a **frock.**

Housewife
—————————————————————*Then*

A **housewife** or **huswife**, in addition to signifying the wife of the house, was a term for a sewing kit, often made up from scraps of fabric sewn together and fitted out to carry a woman's sewing equipment—needles, thread, thimbles, and such. Since women frequently went to one another's houses to sew, this portable case, which could be rolled up to fit into a pocket, proved convenient. Housewives were often beautifully embroidered and finished to show off a woman's handiwork.

Now

A **housewife** is a woman who stays home and cares for her family as distinguished from one who works outside the home.

Linens
Then

Weavers wove various widths of fine **linen** cloth from the flax thread that the women had spun. From the linen cloth, the women then sewed sheets, pillowcases, bolsters, napkins, board cloths, tablecloths, petticoats, aprons, shirts, and other items for their families. Anna Winslow wrote to her mother in March 1772:

> *My aunt gives her love to you & directs me to tell you that she tho't my piece of linnin would have made me a dozen of shifts but she could cut no more than ten out of it. There is some left, but not enough for another. Nine of them are finish'd wash'd & iron'd; & the other would have been long since done if my fingers had not been sore.*[8]

Though the early colonists made linen cloth, having brought with them from England the knowledge of how to grow and prepare flax, spin linen thread and weave linen cloth, they also imported great quantities of linen. Then in the early 1700s a large number of Scotch-Irish Presbyterians, fleeing persecution by the Anglicans, came to New England bringing with them their highly developed skills working with flax; they established a thriving linen industry, centered in Londonderry, New Hampshire, and spreading out from there.

In the mid-nineteenth century, the Reverend Parker wrote of their contribution:

> *These settlers … introduced the art of manufacturing linen*
> *of superior quality, the materials for which they brought with*
> *them … The spinning wheel turned by the foot, which came into*
> *general use, they first brought into the country, and it proved of*
> *essential service to the community.*[9]

By the early nineteenth century, the new United States had its own thriving handmade linen industry.

Now

Today **linens** refer to sheets, pillowcases, tablecloths, and napkins that are made of cotton and synthetic fibers as frequently as of linen itself. When cotton became readily available after the invention of the cotton gin in the 1830s, cotton cloth became an economical alternative to linen for making these useful household items, but the word *linens* continued to be used.

Negligee
Then

A **negligee,** a garment in high fashion for many years, was a dress that opened in the front to show the handsomely decorated petticoat underneath. The *Boston Evening Post* in November 1755 advertised, "Horsehair Quilted Coats to wear with Negligees."[10] These gowns could be quite elaborate. In 1785, Abigail Adams wrote to her friend:

> *Trimming is reserved for full dress only, when very large hoops*
> *and negligees with trains three yards long are worn.*[11]

Now

A negligee is a loose dressing gown or robe, usually made of soft, filmy fabric.

Nightgown
Then

A **nightgown** was a loose fitting, flowing gown or robe made in styles for both women and men—women to entertain at home or on visits and men to wear at work. In August 1772, Anna Winslow recorded in her diary:

> The 6 instant Mr Sam[l] Jarvis was married to Miss Suky Peirce, & on the 13th I made her a visit in company with mamma & many others. The bride was dress'd in a white satin night gound.[12]

At night, men most likely slept in their shirts and women in their shifts.

Now

A **nightgown** is a sleeping garment worn by women.

Petticoat
Then

During the eighteenth century, women wore **petticoats**, a term used for both the underskirts and the skirts themselves. When a maidservant ran away from her master, he advertised for her in the *Boston News-Letter* in June 1713:

> Young Servant Woman, named Mary Sutton, of a Low Stature, light hair, has on a light Manto & Pettycoat lin'd with red, or a yellow & white mixt stuffe without lyning ... [13]

A layered petticoat on a fancy gown could be seen from the opening in the front of the gown's skirt, so the top layer might be made of the same material as the gown and decorated with matching

Wealthy woman's gown showing a petticoat. Detail from a colonial revival (late 1800s) illustration entitled Presenting the Bride.

ruffles and trim or with embroidery. On December 19, 1749, this notice appeared in the *Boston Gazette*:

> On the 11th of Nov. last, was stolen out of the Yard of Mr. Joseph
> Coit, Joiner in Boston, living in Cross street, a Woman's Fustian
> Petticoat, with a large work'd Embroider'd Border, being Deer,
> Sheep, Houses, Forrest, &c., so worked.[14]

In cold weather, quilted petticoats, referred to as "quilts" made of silk and calamanco (fine-glazed wool with sheen), were commonly worn.

Now

A **petticoat** today is a gathered fancy slip worn under a skirt or dress to give the garment fullness.

Pin

Then

*I*n colonial days, **pins** made of metal (often copper) were a necessary part of colonial clothing. A woman might pin a piece of decorative cloth onto the front of her dress, thus wearing what would later be called a pinafore. Long common pins were used to fasten collars and cuffs as well as to secure babies' clothing. Pincushions were a welcome gift to new mothers, as *Poor Robin's Almanack* suggested in 1676:

> Pincushions and such other knacks
> A childbed woman always lacks.[15]

Women ingeniously arranged the pins to be gifted in such a way that the heads emerging from the cushion sent a message to the new arrival. Anna Winslow recounted in her diary:

> My aunt stuck a white sattan pincushin for Mrs Waters. On one
> side, is a planthorn with flowers, on the reverse, just under the
> border are, on one side stuck these words, Josiah Waters, then
> follows on the end, Dec' 1771, on the next side & end are the
> words, Welcome little Stranger.[16]

One that was delivered to a Boston newborn before the Revolutionary War read: "Welcome little Stranger, tho' the Port is closed."[17]

During the Revolutionary War, when pins became scarce, Abigail Adams implored her husband, John, in Philadelphia:

> *I have a request to make you. Something like a Barrel of Sand suppose you will think it, but really of much more importance to me. It is that you would send out Mr. Bass and purchase me a bundle of pins and put in your trunk for me. The cry for pins is so great that what we used to Buy for 7.6 are now 20 Shillings and not to be had for that. A bundle contains 6 thousand for which I used to give a Dollar—but if you can procure them for 50 or 3 pound, pray let me have them.[18]*

Now

A **pin** is a straight, sharp-tipped and capped piece of wire, commonly mass produced, readily available, mostly used in sewing, and easily expendable. We say, "I wouldn't give two pins" for something, meaning that the thing is of scant worth. "Not worth a pin" or "not to care a pin" means the same. A pin is also a piece of jewelry that is pinned on to a dress, blouse, scarf, or coat. **Pin money** is a small amount of money that can be used to buy incidentals.

Pocket

Then

A **pocket** was a bag worn inside a person's clothing, tied around the wearer's waist by a strap frequently made of ribbon or tape. Women carried pockets, sometimes beautifully embroidered, under their skirts throughout the colonial period and well beyond. In the pockets they carried their

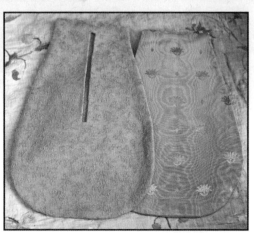

Two reproduction pockets without their ribbons.

fans, handkerchiefs, keys, sewing kits (see *Housewife* above), and more. In addition to pockets, women wore muffs, ruffs, ruffles, and gloves as accessories.

Early in the colonial period, men, too, wore pockets—often leather or fabric pouches—in which they carried coins that were the currency of the day. In 1779, Abner Sanger wrote, "I stop at Washburn's to get cloth for a pocket."[19] As coin money gave way to paper money, men began to use pocketbooks in addition to pockets (see *Pocketbook* in Men and Work).

Now

A **pocket** is a smallish pouch sewn into all sorts of modern-day clothing, with an opening in the garment to provide access.

Tabby

Then

*T*abby was the name colonists gave to silk taffeta material having a wavy, striped, or brindled pattern, the fabric often used for wedding or ball gowns. In addition, as Mercy Warren mentioned in her poem, the colonial women used lawn, a type of muslin cotton cloth, for "widows' caps, cuffs, collars, and frills"; lutestring and Mechlin, silk fabrics with a pleasing glossy sheen; and ducapes, a heavier, soft textured, corded silk, for gowns and petticoats; calamanco, a fine woolen cloth with sheen, to make warmer clothing and bed coverings; and harrateen, a heavy, worsted-wool fabric, for bed curtains and chair upholstery. They also used diaper; holland, a linen cloth; grogram, a mohair or silk/wool weave; tiffany, a transparent silk; alamode, a very thin, usually black silk (used primarily for mourning); and damask, a patterned cloth of worsted wool or silk (used for shoes as well as clothing, window curtains, and upholstery). [20]

Now

Tabby today refers to a striped cat and by extension to all cats.

CLOTHING AND MATERIAL
Chapter Notes:

1   Earle, *Colonial Dames*, 248-249. See *Tabby* for definitions of materials mentioned in the poem. A cardinal was a red cloak. A stomacher was a triangular piece of cloth, sometimes decorated, worn over a woman's chest as the front part of, but not attached to, her gown.

2   Earle, *Customs and Fashions*, 322.

3   Earle, *Customs and Fashions*, 22-23.

4   Dow, *Arts and Crafts*, 158. For definitions of materials, see Tabby.

5   Dow, *Arts and Crafts*, 169.

6   Dow, *Arts and Crafts*, 189.

7   Dow, *Arts and Crafts*, 176.

8   *Diary of Anna Green Winslow*, 47.

9   *Linen-Making*, 14.

10   *Diary of Anna Green Winslow*, 100.

11   *Diary of Anna Green Winslow*, 100.

12   *Diary of Anna Green Winslow*, 67, 118.

13   Dow, *Arts and Crafts*, 185.

14   Dow, *Arts and Crafts*, 176.

15   Earle, *Child Life*, 12.

16   *Diary of Anna Green Winslow*, 12.

17   Earle, *Child Life*, 12.

18   Hogan, 62-63.

19   Ulrich and Stabler, 27.

20   Definitions and quote from Montgomery, *Textiles*, 307, 283, 227, 185, 256-257, 258, 250, 366, 143-144, 213-214.

ORDINARIES, TAVERNS, AND DRINK

Tap room of the Golden Ball Tavern.

*T*he colonial ordinaries, taverns, and inns were initially licensed and sanctioned by the local communities because, even more important than providing drink, food, and lodging for travelers, they provided a place for the town's worshipers to go for "nooning"—the break in the daylong Sunday religious service. At the tavern, parishioners could find warmth in the winter and refreshment in the summer, and always alcoholic beverages, with drink in colonial days being considered a healthy, necessary part of everyday life. One 1702 New England Almanac noted:

> *The days are short, the weather's cold*
> *By tavern fires tales are told*
> *Some ask for dram when first come in*
> *Others with flip or bounce begin.* [1]

City taverns were also where much of the business of the community took place, as Edwin Lasseter Bynner wrote in the 1800s of the taverns of the prior century:

> *They were the centres of so much of its life and affairs, the*
> *resort at once of judge and jury, of the clergy and the laity, of*
> *the politician and the merchant; where the selectmen came to*
> *talk over the affairs of the town, and higher officials to discuss*

the higher interests of the province; where royal governors and distinguished strangers were entertained alike with the humblest wayfarer and the meanest citizen; where were held the carousals of roistering red-coat officers, and the midnight plottings of muttering stern-lipped patriots; where, in fine, the swaggering ensign of the royal army, the frowning Puritan, the … Quaker, the Huguenot refugee, and the savage Indian chief from the neighboring forest might perchance jostle each other in the common taproom.[2]

And another observer added:

The taverns of Boston were the original business Exchanges; they combined the Counting House, the Exchange-office, the Reading-room, and the Bank.[3]

Public notice of court session to be held at a public house.; the Boston Gazette and Country Journal, *December 18, 1775.*

Whether grand city taverns or more humble town or country taverns, these public houses offered both locals and travelers a place to bring and get news and gossip, to read or have newspapers read to them (though the first Boston newspaper did not appear until the early 1700s), and to discuss and debate the politics of the day over a drink. As such, these establishments came to play a significant role in mobilizing popular resistance to the Loyalists and to the British in the years leading up to the Revolutionary War.

Beverage or beverige
Then

*B*everige was the word used in colonial days for any of several weak, watery, alcoholic drinks, such as those made from water poured over the pulp of grapes after the wine had been made or water poured over the remains in the cider mill after the cider had been drawn off. Woe be to the goodwife who provided only such poor drink for her family:

*Beare is indeed in some places constantly drunken, in other
some nothing but Water or Milk, and Water or Beverige; and
that is where the good-wives (if I may so call them) are negligent
and idle; for it is not want of Corn to make Malt with, for the
Country affords enough, but because they are slothful and
careless; and I hope this Item will shame them out of these
humours; that they will be adjudged by their drinke, what kind
of Housewives they are. [4]*

Now

A **beverage**, with modern spelling, refers to any of a variety of liquids drunk
for refreshment.

Bumper

Then

A **bumper** was a
drinking glass
filled full to the brim
with wine or liquor,
usually used to drink a
toast. The bumper had
a thick, heavy bottom
that, when slammed
down on the tavern
table, made a distinct
sound announcing that
the glass was empty.
Unaware of the concept
of germs, colonists
passed the bumper
around and all drank
from the same vessel.
Along with bumpers,
wine and flip glasses,
and small sneakers of

Eighteenth century tavern liquor jug and bottles.

Tavern glasses and mugs.

glass, colonists had drinking vessels made of all sorts of material including gourds, horn, and leather. They had noggins made of wood; tankards, jugs and mugs made of glazed redware, stoneware, or pewter; punch bowls made of ceramics; and beakers, flagons, wine bowls, posset-cups, and flasks made of silver.

Now

Today, **bumper** is generally used along with another word connoting something abundant or unusually large, as in a *bumper crop*.

Cider

Then

The settlers had brought cuts and seeds of English apple trees with them when they came, and within a number of years, apple trees—over thirty different types—grew in abundance in the northern colonies. To the colonists' delight, when planted and nurtured, these cuts and seeds sometimes produced entirely new and delicious types of apples. The Russett, the Pippin, the Baldwin, and the Rhode Island Greening all were unique to New England. Colonists pressed much of their apple crop into **cider** from July to September, first by hand and later by crude mills; but with no facilities

Late eighteenth century Chinese export cider jug. From a private collection.

for refrigeration, the juice quickly fermented into hard cider. Foaming pitchers of the liquor would grace the family table morning, noon, and night, for this was the common drink of women, children, men, laborers, ministers, everyone. *Dramming*, the practice of taking a drink of hard cider midmorning and midafternoon, was an accepted part of men's lives. In Weston, Massachusetts, a 1784 inventory of the town's 105 households showed 1,219 barrels of cider, averaging more than ten barrels per home.[5]

Strange as it may sound to us today, liquor was considered an important part of a child's diet as well in the 1700s, but only at its appropriate time, as this almanac advised parents. In addition to making sure that their beer was warmed, it counseled that it was:

> *Best to feed them on Milk, Pottage, Flummery, Bread, and*
> *Cheese, and not let them drink their beer till they have first eaten*
> *a piece of Brown Bread.*[6]

Without cider, wine and beer, John Adams, still attending the Continental Congress in May of 1777, feared for his health:

> *I would give Three Guineas for a Barrell of your Cyder—not*
> *one drop is to be had here for Gold. And wine is not to be had*
> *under Six or Eight Dollars a Gallon and that very bad. I would*
> *give a Guinea for a Barrell of your Beer. The small beer here*
> *is wretchedly bad. In short I can get nothing that I can drink,*
> *and I believe I shall be sick from this Cause alone. Rum at forty*
> *shillings a Gallon and bad Water, will never do, in this hot*
> *Climate in summer where Acid Liquors are necessary against*
> *Putrefaction.*[7]

Now

Cider, commonly drunk in America, is the juice from pressed apples and other fruits that is refrigerated to prevent hardening. Hard cider, sold as an alcoholic beverage, is once again gaining in popularity.

Coffeehouse
Then

*I*n the early 1700s in Boston, New York, and Philadelphia, **coffeehouses** were public houses that offered the newly imported drink, coffee. They were often large establishments where merchants conducted their business. A bill of fare at a common city coffeehouse would include breakfast, dinner, tea and coffee, supper, lodging, wine, porter (a kind of stout), punch, gin, brandy, housekeeping, and oats (oats for the horses).

In 1759, Mrs. Ballard announced the opening of her coffeehouse three miles from Providence, Rhode Island. Her ad in the *Boston Evening Post* read:

> *For the Entertainment of Gentlemen, Benefit of Commerce, and*
> *Dispatch of Business, a Coffee House is this day opened in King*

> Street. All the Newspapers upon the Continent are regularly taken in,
> and several English Prints and Magazines are ordered. Gentlemen
> who are pleased to use the House, may at any Time of Day, after
> the manner of those in London, have Tea, Coffee, or Chocolate, and
> constant Attendance given by Their humble Servant Mary Ballard[8]

A coffeehouse might even serve as a place to arrange a meeting with a prospective bride as noted in this unusual Boston newspaper notice in 1757:

> To the Ladies. Any young Lady between the Age of Eighteen and
> twenty three of a Middling Stature; brown Hair, regular Features and
> a Lively Brisk Eye: Of Good Morals & not Tinctured with anything
> that may Sully so Distinguishable a Form possessed of 3 or 400£
> entirely her own Disposal and where there will be no necessity of
> going Through the tiresome Talk of addressing Parents or Guardians
> for their consent: Such a one by leaving a Line directed for A. W.
> at the British Coffee House in King Street appointing where an
> Interview may be had will meet with a Person who flatters himself he
> shall not be thought Disagreeable by any Lady answering the above
> description. N. B. Profound Secrecy will be observ'd. No Trifling
> Answers will be regarded.[9]

Soon fine taverns in the outlying towns offered their guests coffee as well, but without changing the name of the establishments to coffeehouses.

John Adams found this out when he stopped at a tavern one afternoon much in need of a cup of tea after he had just ridden more than thirty-five miles:

> "Madam" said I to Mrs. Huston, "is it lawfull for a weary Traveller
> to refresh himself with a Dish of Tea provided it has been honestly
> smuggled, or paid no Duties?"

> "No sir, said she, we have renounced all Tea in this place. I cant make
> Tea, but I'le make you Coffee." Accordingly I have drank Coffee every
> Afternoon since, and have borne it very well. Tea must be universally
> renounced. I must be weaned, and the sooner, the better.[10]

Now

A **coffeehouse** has evolved in the twenty-first century from a place where people used to go now and then to have a cup of coffee or tea and a pastry, and perhaps listen to poetry or jazz, to a place where people go daily to get their fix of espresso, cappuccino, half-caf soy-milk latte or whatever particular light or dark, South American or African coffee or tea blends they desire. Starbucks, Peets, Seattle's Best, and many other coffeehouses cater to the customer's every wish.

Entertainment
Then

*I*n colonial days, **entertainment** had a special meaning for taverns and ordinaries: It meant providing food, drink, and lodging for travelers. In 1652 in Cambridge, Massachusetts, Andrew Belcher and his wife were "granted the liberty to sell beer and bread for entertainment of strangers and the good of the town." [11]

Inkeepers, Ordinaries, Tipling, Drunkennes.

FOR as much as there is a necessary use of houses of Common-entertainment, in every Common wealth and of such as retaile wine, beer, and victuals, yet because there are so many abuses, both by persons entertaining, and by persons entertained, It is therefore Ordered by this Court and Authority thereof, That no person or persons shall at any time, under any pretence or Colour whatsoever, undertake to be a Common victualer, keeper of a Cooks shop, or house for Common entertainment Taverner or publick seller of wine, Ale, beer or strong-waters, by retaile, (nor shall any sell wine privately in his house, or out of doores, by a less quantity then a quarter caske) without approbation of the Selected Townsmen, and Licence of the County Court, where they dwell, upon pain of forfeiture of *five pounds*, for every such offence; or imprisonment at the pleasure of the Court. Provided it shall be Lawfull for any whole-sale Merchant of wines, or the present Stillers of strong waters, being Masters of families, or such as receive the same from Forraine parts. In cases &c: or makers of Cyder, to sell by retaile; Provided the quantity of wine and cyder, be not less then three gallons at a time, to one person, nor strong waters less then a quart; and that it be only to masters of families of good and honest report, or persons going to Sea, and they suffer not any person to drink the same in their houses, cellars or yards. F 2

Law regulating public houses.

Taverns and ordinaries were required by law to provide such entertainment for both man and beast. Thus their bill of fare would include oats as well as breakfast, lunch, dinner, and drink. In William Ellery's diary of his travels to and from the Continental Congress, he wrote, "we lodged in clean beds, free from Bugs, and our horses were well entertained." [12]

On the other hand, these establishments were prohibited from offering activities that would be thought of as entertainment today. The 1692 license granted to an Andover landlord, whose establishment was called "by the sign of the Horse Shoe," specified:

> *Whereas the above said William Chandler is admitted and*
> *allowed by their Majesties' Justices at a General Sessions of the*
> *Peace to keep a common Home of Entertainment and to use*

Tavern dice cups.

common selling of Ale, Beer, Syder,
etc., ... the said William Chandler,
during the time of keeping a Public
House, shall not permit, suffer, or have
any playing at Dice, Cards, Tables,
Quoits, Loggets, Bowls, Ninepins,
Billiards, or any other unlawful Game
or Games in his House, yard, Garden,
or Backside ... ."[13]

Dancing too was prohibited. In 1631, the
Massachusetts Bay magistrates ordered
that in "consequence of some miscarriages
at weddings"[14] (the wording raises some
interesting speculations), dancing was
hereafter banned in public houses.
Evidence indicates, though, that despite the
proscription, dancing as well as cards and other games flourished in taverns.

Now

Entertainment today is simply any form of activity or recreation—games,
theater, television, sports—from which the participant or viewer derives
pleasure or amusement.

Grog
Then

*G*rog to the colonists connoted watered-down liquor. William Ellery,
finding himself in a dangerous situation in his travels to and from the
Continental Congress during the Revolutionary War, wrote:

> In the first Place we fortified our Stomachs with Beef Steak and
> Grogg, and then went to work to fortify ourselves against an
> Attack.[15]

Grog is said to have originated in the 1740s when British Admiral Edward
Vernon, a popular naval captain, ordered that the rum ration given to his
men aboard ship be watered down, in hopes of diluting the drink as well

as the number of drunken fights among his men. Admiral Vernon was nicknamed "Old Grogram" because of his habit of wearing a grogram (coarse material of silk and hair) cloak; in time, the nickname was shortened to Old Grog, and the drink he fashioned was called grog.[16]

Now——————————————————————

Grog today is still enjoyed as a drink, though primarily by colonial re-enactors. Made in a variety of different ways, it usually includes rum as a base. The word *groggy* equates with dazed, hung over, or slightly intoxicated.

Hobnob
————————————————————————*Then*

To **hobnob**, hob a nob, or hob and nob, was to toast one another's health, sometimes to toast one another alternately and, later, to imbibe convivially. It has also been said that a hobnob was the name given the stone projection built into the brick side of the enormous fireplace in the colonial kitchen. Here, after the cooking and cleaning were done and the fire banked, two family members might sit and visit (thus, *hobnob*) with one another in the warmth of the gently glowing coals.

Now——————————————————————

To **hobnob** is to visit and/or converse familiarly with someone.

Landlord
————————————————————————*Then*

Tavern keepers in colonial days were called **landlords.** The Puritan magistrates selected sober respectable men of means to be landlords, believing that they were best suited to provide the service to the community without looking first to their own interests. When tavern keeping became a business like any other, the court of sessions kept a degree of control over the landlords' behavior by requiring them to be licensed and, as the law of 1741 made clear to the licensing boards of the towns:

It's expected of you, that whenever you shall judge meet to approve any new Taverner or Retailer in your Town, you do recommend him as a Person

Isaac Jones receives his innholder's license in 1770.

of sober Conversation, suitably qualified and provided for the Exercise of such an Employment, agreeable to Law.[17]

Local law regulated the amount of liquor that the landlord could sell, to whom and when he could sell it, and what else he could or could not do. A 1692 Andover license spelled out the limitations clearly:

Nor shall sell any Wine or Liquors to any Indians or Negroes nor suffer any apprentices or servants or any other persons to remain in his house tippling or drinking after nine of the Clock at night time; nor buy or take to Pawn any stolen goods, nor willingly Harbor in his said House, Barn, Stable, or Otherwhere any Rogues, Vagabonds, Thieves, nor any other notorious offenders whatsoever … and in his said house shall and do use and maintain good order and Rule … .[18]

While some widows were allowed to keep taverns as a means to support themselves and their families, landlords, for the most part, continued to be prominent male members of their communities, often selectmen, representatives to the general court, and/or militia officers. In 1771, John Adams wrote of the landlord of a tavern in Enfield, Connecticut:

Oated and drank tea at Peases—a smart house and landlord truly; well dressed with his ruffles, &c. and upon inquiry I found he was the great man of the town, their representative as well as tavern-keeper.[19]

Now

A **landlord** is a person who owns or runs a boarding house or inn or a person who rents space or land to a tenant.

Loggerhead

Then

*I*n a colonial tavern, a **loggerhead,** also known as a flip dog, was an iron poker with a bulbous end that was heated red-hot in the taproom fire. The glowing end was thrust into a glass of flip, a popular tavern drink, to sear the sweetener and foam the beverage. One poet wrote:

> *Landlord, to thy bar room skip,*
> *Make it a foaming mug of flip*
> *Make it of our country's staple,*
> *Rum, New England sugar maple,*
> *Beer that's brewed from hops and Pumpkins,*
> *Hark! I hear the poker sizzle*
> *And O'er the mug the liquor drizzle*
> *And against the earthen mug*
> *I hear the wooden spoon's cheerful dub.*[20]

And another:

> *Where dozed a fire of beechen logs that bred*
> *Strange fancies in its embers golden-red,*
> *And nursed the loggerhead, whose hissing dip,*
> *Timed by nice instinct, creamed the bowl of flip.*[21]

If a political or personal argument at a tavern became heated, and well it might as the opponents became increasingly inebriated, the parties might be moved to seize and brandish the red-hot loggerheads, taking jabs at one another. Certainly, they could be said to be "at loggerheads."

Two other possible origins present themselves for the expression "to be at loggerheads." Large heated loggerheads were used by tars (sailors) to melt pitch or tar. Sailors brandishing these as weapons, and ready to throw hot tar at one another, were said to be at loggerheads. Loggerheads were also used as ramrods aboard ships to pack the explosives into the barrels of the large mounted guns. Once the

Loggerhead.

enemy had boarded the ship, the sailors would be left to defend themselves *at loggerheads.*

To call a man a loggerhead was to say he was an ignorant blockhead.

Now

To be at **loggerheads** means to be at an angry stalemate in an argument with another person.

Mind your p's and q's
Then

The colonial tavern keeper is said to have marked on a board the letters *P* and *Q* to keep track of the pints and quarts drunk add by each of his visitors. If a man was drinking to excess, the tavern keeper might warn him: "**Mind your p's and q's.**"

Rise of the Spirit of Independence

The printer's shop may have been another source of the expression. In colonial days, the printer's apprentices, called devils, had to place each piece of metal type into the frame to form the words and sentences, paragraphs and columns that, when inked and pressed onto paper, became the printed piece. Frequently these young people would confuse the p's and q's especially in the dim light in which they worked, and so would be admonished, "Mind your p's and q's."

Now

Mind your p's and q's means to mind your manners, to be on your best behavior.

Ordinary

Then

*A*n **ordinary** (used as a noun) in colonial days was a home licensed by the local government to provide food, liquor, and lodging to travelers and townspeople. It was called an ordinary because the visitor partook of the ordinary meal prepared and offered to them at a set time for a set price. In some, one room in the house was made into a taproom, sometimes itself called an ordinary, where visitors could purchase liquor and partake of their meals. The liquor was served from behind a bar built into a corner of the room. The bar could be locked when unattended thus protecting the expensive and heavily taxed drink from pilferage.

Replica of tavern bar.

Local authorities closely supervised the sale of liquor. One chagrined customer in the early 1600s complained:

> *At the houses of entertainment called ordinaries into which a stranger went, he was presently followed by one appointed to that office who would thrust himself into his company uninvited, and if he called for more drink than the officer thought, in his judgment, he could soberly bear away, he would presently countermand it, and appoint the proportion beyond which he could not get one drop.*[22]

Tavern lantern.

Also called taverns or inns, the ordinaries served an important role in the community as public houses. They were the only places where travelers could expect to purchase a bed for the night (no matter how primitive or unclean, and no matter how many other people already occupied that room or, indeed, that bed.) Ordinaries and taverns were also the only heated, lighted (some finer taverns having twenty or more candlesticks) social centers in which townspeople could gather formally or informally for conviviality or for private or town-sanctioned events. Everything from trials to business meetings, religious to social celebrations, cock fights to puppet shows, mail pickup to stagecoach stops took place there. Militia musters, frequently held at or near the tavern or ordinary, ended inside with a glass of flip or a tankard of beer.

The ordinary was also the place where information was gathered and shared. In 1777, the British soldier Thomas Anburey told of his friend's annoyance at being constantly badgered for news whenever "he travelled from his own province to Boston, and alighted at an ordinary, (the name given to inns in America, and some justly merit that title)." [23]

It is said that these establishments often had boxes nailed to the wall of the taproom for visitors to leave gratuities for the servants. The boxes sported the initials TIP standing for To Insure Promptness.

Now

Ordinary today retains only the colonial sense of unexceptional or usual.

Tavern
Then

A **tavern** was another name for an ordinary or inn (see above). Taverns varied in quality from the most modest and mean (usually located near the waterfront or in rural areas) to the most luxurious and genteel (often found in larger cities and towns). Taverns came to play an important role in the run-up to the American Revolution. Each tavern in a town had its own political flavor

Side entrance of Golden Ball Tavern.

according to the leanings of the tavern keeper, and townspeople gathered in their preferred establishments to discuss the news and politics of the day over a drink.

Certain taverns, such as the Bunch of Grapes and the Green Dragon Tavern in Boston, were gathering places for the Patriot leaders where they planned their course of resistance to British laws and regulations. These meetings were often held in upstairs chambers so that the conversations could not be overheard. Others, such as the Golden Ball Tavern in Weston, Massachusetts, were known as

Loyalist taverns. In 1775, when General Gage's spies stopped at the Golden Ball Tavern on their travels to map the best route to capture the Patriots' stores of military supplies in Worcester and Concord, the tavern keeper Isaac Jones signaled his loyalty

Notice of celebratory dinner held at the Bunch of Grapes Tavern, in Continental Journal and Weekly Advertiser, *November 8, 1781.*

to the Crown by offering the visitors tea, a commodity banned by the Patriots. The spies noted in their diary, "We immediately found out with whom we were, and were not a little pleased ... to find that he was a friend to government."[24]

Now

A **tavern** is a local place to go to have a beer or a drink and eat a meal. Its role as a place for political discussion per se is no longer so prominent as in colonial times.

Ordinaries, Taverns, and Drink
Chapter Notes:

1   Conroy, 46.

2   Earle, *Stage-Coach and Tavern Days,* 196-197.

3   Earle, *Stage-Coach and Tavern Days,* 199.

4   Earle, *Stage-Coach and Tavern Days,* 131-132.

5   Dickson and Lucas, 25-26.

6   Earle, *Customs and Fashions,* 24.

7   Butterfield, ed., 174.

8   Dexter, 12-13.

9   Earle, *Custom and Fashions,* 66.

10   Butterfield, ed., 61.

11   Forbes and Eastman, *Taverns and Stagecoaches,* vol. I, 111.

12   Ellery, 480.

13   Earle, *Stage-Coach and Tavern Days,* 64-65.

14   Earle, *Stage-Coach and Tavern Days,* 5-6.

15   Ellery, 322.

16   Mack, 255.

17   Isaac Jones Family Papers.

18   Earle, *Stage-Coach and Tavern Days,* 65-66.

19   Earle, *Customs and Fashions,* 196.

20   Crawford, 143.

21   Earle, *Customs and Fashions,* 209.

22   Earle, *Customs and Fashions,* 165.

23   Anburey, *Travels,* vol. 2, 69.

24   Gambrill, 23.

POLITICS

*F*rom the moment the colonists set sail aboard the *Mayflower*, they occupied themselves with fundamental political issues. They needed to construct their own governing bodies and rules and to decide who could vote and who would govern. They chose a system that proved sufficiently effective to last until today in New England, that of the town meetings at which eligible, in those days only male, residents elected the selectmen, selected the minister, and even helped establish the laws and regulations to govern the town.

In the early 1800s, the New Haven minister and president of Yale College, Timothy Dwight, lauded their accomplishments:

> *The colonization of a wilderness by civilized men, where a regular government, mild manners, arts, learning, science, and Christianity have been interwoven in its progress from the beginning, is a state of things of which the eastern continent and the records of past ages furnish neither an example, nor a resemblance.* [1]

Far from the heavy hand of the king, British Parliament, and aristocracy, these early settlers planted the seeds of a more democratic system. So, for instance, it was the members of the town who decided on the taxes that townspeople would pay. Steeped in this pattern of participatory government, New Englanders, not surprisingly, balked in the 1760s and 1770s at British regulations seeking to impose taxes on them without their consent.

Caucus
Then

*C*aucuses of the various political factions met frequently in the period before the American Revolution to plan their strategies. In 1788, an historian of the Revolution wrote:

> *The word caucus ... and its derivative caucusing, are often used in Boston ... . It seems to mean a number of persons,*

> *whether more or less, met together to consult upon adopting*
> *and prosecuting some scheme of policy for carrying a favourite*
> *point ... . More than fifty years ago, Mr. Samuel Adams's father*
> *and twenty others, one or two from the north end of the town,*
> *where all the ship-business is carried on, used to meet, to make*
> *a Caucus, and lay their plan for introducing certain persons*
> *into places of trust and power. When they had settled it, they*
> *separated, and used each their particular influence within his*
> *own circle.*[2]

Well before colonial days, the Algonquin tribe used the term *cau-cau-a-su* to mean *adviser*. Some say that the colonists, learning that the Indian leaders used the term for their powwows, applied it to their own political meetings. Others suggest, as noted in the above quote, that since some members of the Caucus Club came from the North End where ship building was a prominent trade, the word *caucus* may have derived from meetings held before the 1730s by disgruntled ship *caulkers* meeting to discuss their grievances.

Now

A **caucus** is a political group organized to achieve a particular end, such as nominating a political candidate or deciding on a party platform. The verb form means to meet by sides during negotiations. In 1816, John Pickering, author of *Vocabulary, or Collection of Words and Phrases Which Have Been Supposed to be Peculiar to the United States of America,* made it clear that caucus was not a respectable word. "It need hardly be remarked, that this *cant* word and its derivatives are never used in good writing."[3] *Cant* was the word for the language of "Gypsies, Beggers [sic], Thieves, Cheats, &c."[4]

Council
Then

*I*n early colonial days, a **council** was an official meeting with a group of Native Americans to talk over boundaries, treaties, and other matters. Describing the progress of his trip home from Philadelphia in January of 1776, John Adams wrote to Abigail:

*I waited on General Thomas at Roxbury this Morning, and
then went to Cambridge where I dined at Coll. Mifflins with the
General, and Lady, and a vast Collection of other Company,
among whom were six or seven Sachems and Warriours, of the
French Cagnawaga Indians, with several of their Wives and
Children. A savage Feast they made of it, yet were very polite in
the Indian style … .*

*I was introduced to them by the General as one of the grand
Council Fire at Philadelphia, which made them prick up their
Ears, they came and shook Hands with me, and made me low
Bows, and scrapes &c. In short I was much pleased with this
Days entertainment.*[5]

Now

A **council** is a group of people meeting to deliberate an issue, or an elected
or appointed group meeting in an advisory, legislative, or administrative
capacity.

Red tape
Then

*I*n the seventeenth and eighteenth centuries, British official documents
came tied with a red woolen tape. As the colonists' anger grew over
increasingly oppressive British regulations, **red tape** took on an ever
more negative connotation. The last straw came in 1775 when the British
Parliament passed and sent to the colonies the American Prohibitory Act
known as the Restraining Act, which proscribed all American shipping and
sale of American goods abroad. The colonists had had enough of the red
tape and enough of Britain's oppressive rule. John Adams rejoiced:

*The late Act of Parliament, has made so deep an Impression
upon Peoples Minds throughout the Colonies, it is looked upon
as the last Stretch of Oppression, that We are hastening rapidly
to great Events. Governments will be up every where before
Midsummer, and an End to Royal style, Titles and Authority.
Such mighty Revolutions make a deep Impression on the Minds
of Men and sett many violent Passions at Work. Hope, Fear, Joy,*

Sorrow Love, Hatred, Malice, Envy, Revenge, Jealousy, Ambition, Avarice, Resentment, Gratitude, and every other Passion, Feeling, Sentiment, Principle and Imagination, were never in more lively Exercise than they are now, from Florida to Canada inclusively.[6]

Now

Red tape connotes excessively complex, time-consuming procedures, regulations, and forms. In the early 1800s, Washington Irving vented his frustrations at a petty official by writing, "His brain was little better than red tape and parchment."[7]

Riot act
Then

*I*n 1715, the British passed into law the **Riot Act**, which held that whenever a group of twelve or more people congregated unlawfully and were deemed to be disturbing the peace, a proclamation was to be read. If upon

the reading of the proclamation the crowd did not disperse, its members would be held guilty of a felony.

When, in 1773, to protest the despised British Tea Act, which gave a virtual monopoly to the British East India company to import and have their agents sell tea in the colonies, a group of Boston Patriots decided to act to prevent the offloading of the tea from ships lying in Boston harbor, John Adams must have known well that the Patriots were violating the riot act. A gang, disguised as Indians, boarded the British ships to dump "3 Cargoes of Bohea Tea" into the sea that December night. But even while Adams pondered, "What Measures will the Ministry take, in Consequence of this?" he exulted:

This is the most magnificent Movement of all … . I cant but consider it as an Epocha in History… . To let [the tea] be landed, would be giving up the Principle of Taxation by Parliamentary

Authority, against which the Continent have struggled for 10 years."[8]

Parliament did more than prosecute the perpetrators as felons in violation of the Riot Act. In March 1774, it passed the Boston Port Act, also known as the Intolerable Acts, closing the port of Boston, and it sent General Gage as military governor to enforce a series of coercive acts designed to bring Boston to its knees.

Now

To read the **riot act** means to loudly and emphatically warn or scold. Many parents must feel sympathy for the British whose Riot Act was about as effective as theirs today. The British did not repeal the Riot Act until 1967.

Stamp
Then

When the British passed the Stamp Act in 1765, their intent was to tax the colonists by requiring that all colonial legal documents, almanacs, broadsides, newspapers, even diplomas and playing cards be printed on paper that bore the embossed royal imprint ensuring that the fee had been paid before the document was printed. The colonists were outraged, and the act actually had the effect of further uniting the colonists in their resistance to British laws. One printer defiantly printed his newspaper with a banner that read: "**LIBERTY** and **PROPERTY,** and **NO STAMPS**."[9]

In colonial days, there were, for the most part, no such things as the small squares or rectangles, with images on the front and glue on the back, to be applied as paid postage to letters or documents. If

"*Mary Pelham presents her Compliments to the Person who took a letter last week from the Post Office, and if they have sufficiently examined the contents, she will be much obliged to them, if they will either return it to the Post Master, or leave It at her house in Cambridge-Street, as she wishes to peruse it herself.*" From the Continental Journal and Weekly Advertiser, *November 1, 1781.*

the sender of the letter chose to have his message carried by one of the post riders rather than a traveling friend or neighbor, the fee was usually paid by the recipient. The cost of posting a letter depended on the number of sheets of paper plus the distance that the letter had traveled. Each additional sheet doubled the cost, so none but the very wealthy used envelopes. Instead, letter writers used sheets of paper folded over, addressed and sealed with sealing wax. People, it also appears, were not averse to taking and reading other people's mail as a way of getting news.

Now

A **stamp** is the well-known small square or rectangle with an image on the front and adhesive on the backside, to be affixed to the top right corner of an envelope for mailing letters or documents. The first postage stamps, then called labels, appeared in 1847. As in colonial days, a stamp is also an implement that when inked can be used to make a mark or sign.

Stump
Then

*I*n 1716, in *Memories of a Huguenot Family,* Ann Maury tells of a colonist bringing the word **stump** back from a Saponi tribal town in Virginia. There he had seen the large stump of a tree in the center of the village. When he asked why the stump was still there, he was told that the Saponi leader used it as a platform from which to talk to his people.[9] The term stump caught on since it captured in a word the act of a politician or partisan giving a stump speech, exhorting a gathered crowd to heed and agree with his position.

There was also a 1775 song about George Washington that went, "Upon a stump he placed himself, George Washington, he did."

Now

Stump is a word for the action of a political incumbent or candidate who goes around his or her district delivering a political message to voters. He or she can be said to be "on the stump."

POLITICS
Chapter Notes:

1 Dwight, *Travels*, vol. I, 6. Dwight also remarks, "When they came to America, they believed themselves, and were often declared by the Crown, to bring with them all the rights of Englishmen..." vol. I, 119.

2 Pickering, 56.

3 Pickering, 57.

4 *The First English Dictionary of Slang*, 1699, title page.

5 Butterfield, ed., 114.

6 Butterfield, ed., 126.

7 Morris, 483.

8 Butterfield, ed., 53.

9 Jaffe, 53.

10 Morris, 548.

MILITARY

*N*ew England colonial militias were made up of military-age men required to serve in trained bands. These trained bands had long existed in the colonies to protect against the many threats from the Indians, the French, and the Dutch. What distinguished them from their European counterparts was that they trained and regulated themselves, electing their own officers and all sharing in the decision-making. Although the units were originally formed to defend the interests of the British Crown, by 1775 most members had retracted their pledge to support the British and had pledged instead to support the revolutionary government. Some towns chose to form "minute companies," drawn from already existing militia units, with the Minutemen ready to take up arms on short notice, while others chose to train and arm as before. All now shared an interest in defending their "country, Priveledges and Libertys."[1] Years after the war, one of these citizen-soldiers was asked by an historian why he had gone to war. Was it because of the Stamp Act? The tea tax? The writings of John Locke and others on liberty? No, he replied:

Statue of Lexington Minuteman.

> *Young man, what we meant in going for those Redcoats was this:*
> *we always had governed ourselves and we always meant to. They*
> *didn't mean we should.*[2]

*A*larm

Then

*A*larm was used as a verb meaning to warn or to notify of impending danger. John Adams wrote that on the morning of April 19, 1775, the British marched from Boston: "The men appointed to alarm the country on such occasions … took their different routes."[3] The men he was speaking of were Paul Revere, William Dawes, Dr. Samuel Prescott, and others who had been delegated to ride out to warn and mobilize the people in the towns around Boston. Prescott reached Concord, had the bell rung, and rode off to wake the militia and to warn the Reverend William Emerson. In his diary, Emerson wrote:

This morning between 1 and 2 o'clock we were alarmed by the ringing of the bell, and upon examination found that the troops to the number of 800, had stole their march from Boston in boats and barges."[4]

Thus *alarmed*, the towns surrounding Boston were all put on alert and their militias joined forces to repel the British. Alarmed was also used as an adjective meaning to be frightened.

Now

Alarm as a verb is most often used to mean to frighten or to be frightened. To *sound an alarm* today means to warn.

Flash in the pan

Then

*B*y an Act for Regulating the Militia published in the *Boston News-Letter*, February 7/14, 1773/4, each soldier

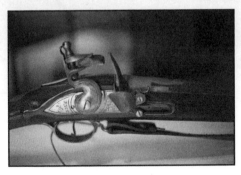

Firing mechanism of a British Brown Bess musket. Courtesy of Christopher Anderson, colonial furniture maker.

and other Householdler shall be always provided with a well fixt Firelock

Musket, or Musket or Bastard-Musket bore, the Barrel not less than three Foot and an half long, or other good Fire Arms to the satisfaction of the Commission Officer of the Company; a Cartouch Box: one Pound of good Powder: Twenty Bullets fit for his Gun, and twelve Flynts; a good Sword or Cutlass; a Worm, & priming Wire, fit for his Gun, on Penalty of six Shillings.[5]

To ready a flintlock musket to fire, the colonial militiaman put a small amount of black powder into the priming pan, a small cupped receptacle on the musket, and then pulled the trigger which released the hammer. The hammer held a piece of flint; when the flint struck against the hardened steel, it created a spark that ignited the priming powder. The explosion from the ignited powder went in to the touchhole at the base of the barrel and ignited the powder charge. This in turn forced the ejection (the shot) of a lead ball out of the barrel. If the touchhole was plugged with residue from the last firing, or if there was insufficient (or even wet) powder when the spark was struck, the powder would ignite in the pan itself without traveling into the barrel to ignite the main charge. The resulting *fizzle* (an onomatopoetic word for the sound it made) was called a **flash in the pan**; no ball would be ejected and the shot would not be completed.

Now

A **flash in the pan** refers to someone or something that does not live up to the initial billing. The person or thing essentially fails before he/she/it can perform as was hoped and expected.

Half-cocked

Then

*I*f the hammer of the early flintlock musket was in the halfway position, or **half-cocked,** it would not fire even when the trigger was pulled. Only at full cock would the weapon fire when the trigger was pulled.

Now

To go off **half-cocked** means to say or do something impulsively and imprudently, without full thought or means to complete the intended action.

Lock, stock, and barrel
Then

In order for a gun to be fully functional, it needed to have all three components: a lock (the firing mechanism), a stock, and a barrel. Many colonial craftsmen and farmers were capable of making the stock of a gun; in fact, many colonists picked up the guns left by the French in the French and Indian War in the mid-1700s and replaced their damaged stocks with new ones made of cherry, walnut or tiger maple. But it took a gunsmith to make the whole— **lock, stock, and barrel**.

One man advertised in the *Boston News-Letter,* in July 1712, that his pistol:

> *Dropt out of the Holster, the barrel having on it the Tower mark, all the other work (except the stock of Maple, and the Lock made by R Lawrence) being handsomely wrought with silver and the London Goldsmith's Hall mark on it.*[6]

British Brown Bess musket. Courtesy of Christopher Anderson, colonial furniture maker.

Now

Lock, stock, and barrel today means the entire thing. To own something lock, stock, and barrel is to own it completely.

Pioneer
Then

A **pioneer** in the colonial military was a foot soldier who was sent ahead of the troops to repair roads, dig trenches, and open the way for the others.

Now ————————————————

A **pioneer** is a person who goes off to settle in unexplored territory or one who is an innovator or forerunner in an endeavor or profession.

To the hilt
———————————————— *Then*

The hilt was the cross bar separating the handle from the blade of a knife or sword. If the weapon were thrust into someone or something up **to the hilt,** that meant the full blade was employed and the stabbing certainly completed.

A British officer's sword. Courtesy of Christopher Anderson, colonial furniture maker.

Now ————————————————

To the hilt means to the utmost, to the limit, completely.

Windage
———————————————— *Then*

In colonial days, **windage** referred to the allowance made for a small additional distance between the ball and the bore of a gun. There had to be windage in the colonial musket because fouling—from debris left from the previous shot—might prevent a tight-fitting ball from being rammed down the barrel when the militiaman needed to rapid-fire. The balls had to be loose fitting enough not to jam. The availability of windage in the colonial muskets helps to explain why they were preferred to rifles in the Revolutionary War. As the colonial militia began to adopt the linear rapid-fire fighting formations of the British with their ranks and rotations, they found that rifles were not as efficient in volley firing as muskets since rifles required more time to load than muskets.

Now

Windage is the allowance a rifleman or marksman has to make for the effect of wind drift on the trajectory of the bullet.

MILITARY

Chapter Notes:

1   Fischer, *Paul Revere's Ride,* 152-153.

2   Fischer, *Paul Revere's Ride,* 163-164.

3   Fischer, *Paul Revere's Ride,* 138.

4   Fischer, *Paul Revere's Ride,* 144.

5   Dow, *Arts and Crafts,* 272.

6   Dow, *Arts and Crafts,* 272.

NAUTICAL

Notice of sailing of the sloop Speedwell, *the* Boston Evening Post, *November 15, 1773.*

The colorful vocabulary of the sea had its origins well before the colonial period, but the words and expressions used then continue to bring their evocative meanings to us today. This was the era of sailing vessels, the single-masted sloop, the double-masted schooner and brig, and the three-masted fully rigged ship and frigate. New Englanders with their ready supply of wood to build ships, their proximity to good harbors and their facility at fishing and trading, were fully involved with ships and shipping. John Adams, himself a lawyer, used a nautical expression when he accused a colleague he thought a "blockhead" of being "ignorant of every Rope in the Ship."[1]

At the start of hostilities with Great Britain, the colonies had no navy. They commandeered and armed colonial merchantmen, and, when those proved nearly useless, the Continental Congress passed a law in the fall of 1775 authorizing the building of an American navy. The new navy would face a formidable foe. Abigail Adams described the scene she observed from her hilltop vantage in Quincy overlooking Boston harbor in March 1776:

> *The Enemy have not yet come under sail. I cannot help suspecting some design which we do not yet comprehend; to what quarter of the World they are bound is wholy unknown, but tis generally Thought to New york [sic] …*

ALL able-bodied Seamen, ordinary Seamen and Landmen, are hereby informed, That the two fine fast-failing Continental Frigates *Alliance* and *Deane*, the first commanded by *John Barry*, Esq; and the other by *Samuel Nicholson*, Esq; are bound in Confort on a Cruife against the Enemy, and will fail soon, with every Prospect of making a very advantageous Cruife. ALL Seamen and others, that incline to enter on board either of said Ships have hereby prefented to them the following great Encouragements and Affurances, which shew the Advantage of this Service to be superior to any other.

The Officers and Crews shall be intitled to the whole of all Veffels of War they shall capture, without any Deduction or Claim from the United States.

Advertisement for seamen published in the Continental Journal and Weekly Advertiser, *November 1, 1781.*

From Pens Hill we have a view of the largest Fleet ever seen in America. You may count upwards of 100 & 70 Sail. They look like a Forrest.[2]

Back and fill
—Then

*I*n colonial days, to **back and fill** meant to maneuver a sailing ship back and forth by alternately filling its sails and then emptying them of wind, to speed the ship up or slow it down in order to enable the captain to steer it safely down a narrow river channel into port.

Now

To **back and fill** means to be ambivalent, to go mentally back and forth, or to vacillate about an issue or decision. In sailing the phrase retains its colonial meaning today.

Bitter end
—Then

*T*he **bitter end** was a nautical term for that part of the ship's anchor cable that remained aboard ship, fastened to the bit or post, when the anchor was let out. In the words of the *Sea-man's Grammar and Dictionary* (1691):

> *A bitter is but the turn of a Cable about the Bits, and veere it out by little and little. And the Bitter end is that part of the cable doth stay within board.*[3]

Now

The **bitter end** is the final point or extremity to which a person would go in dealing with a difficult situation.

Caboose

—Then

The colonial **caboose** was the cookhouse on a merchantman or fishing boat. It was usually located on deck and was often fitted out with a cast-iron cooking range or moveable fireplace, which sometimes shared the name caboose. When his ship broke up in a heavy storm, one lucky sailor floated ashore on a caboose (surely not the cast-iron stove but rather the small box or house covering that apparatus) that had come loose from its home on the forepart of the quarterdeck.

Now

The **caboose** is the car that brings up the rear on freight trains. It is equipped with a kitchen and beds the trainmen can use. Found on all freight trains for most of the eighteenth and nineteenth centuries, cabooses today are far less frequently seen.

Cut of his jib

—Then

In colonial days, sailors could often tell the make of another ship as well as its nationality from the **cut of its jib** or jibs (triangular sails set at the front of the ship) it flew. Different nations used different styles and numbers of jibs, with some using none at all. Armed with this knowledge, sailors could quickly judge whether another ship was friend or foe.

Now

To judge someone by the **cut of his jib** is to judge that person's character and abilities by the first impression he or she makes.

Detail showing (white) jib on the USS Enterprise *from the illustration on the face of a David Wood clock depicting the naval battle between the* Enterprise *and the* Boxer *during the War of 1812. From a private collection.*

Figurehead
————————————————————————*Then*

*T*o the colonists, as to people for centuries, a **figurehead** was the carved wooden ornamental bust or full figure that was affixed to the bow of a sailing ship. It represented the guiding, protective spirit of the vessel.

Most of the numerous large British ships built in New England in the 1600s and 1700s had carved figureheads on their bows. These ornaments were designed and fashioned by a few trained carvers. A Boston carver's bill from 1689 called for a "Lyon," the most common form of figurehead from the 1600s to the mid-1700s when the horse briefly replaced it. By the 1760s, carvers were turning out figureheads of famous people, mythical gods, and women, often representing the name of the ship. So, for instance, the frigate *Hancock*, one of thirteen frigates authorized to be built for the Continental navy in 1775, was ordered to be adorned with an elaborate figurehead of John Hancock, a leading political figure in the Revolution, complete with "yellow Breeches, white stockings, Blue Coat with Yellow Button Holes, Small cocked Hat with a Yellow Lace."[4]

Now————————————————————————

A **figurehead** is the nominal head of an organization or business but one who in reality has no authority or power. It also retains its meaning as the ornamental figure affixed to a ship's prow.

Scuttlebutt
————————————————————————*Then*

*O*n colonial ships, the lidded cask around which the ship's sailors gathered to drink fresh water was called the **scuttlebutt**. It was made of a butt (a large wooden cask), which had a hole made in it (thus *scuttled*) from which the water could flow. As the men stood around drinking, they also surely would share the latest gossip.

Now

Scuttlebutt today refers to the latest gossip or news. In the U.S. Navy, the ship's water fountain still is called a scuttlebutt.

Taken aback
Then

*T*o be **taken aback** was to have the ship suddenly blown backwards when the sails were filled with air blowing directly over the bow (the front of the ship) by shifting winds or heavy seas.

Now

To be **taken aback** is to be surprised or abashed by a piece of news or an occurrence.

SHIPS

Chapter Notes:

1   Butterfield, ed., 63.

2   Butterfield, ed., 118.

3   Quoted from *Seaman's Grammar*, Book I, 30.

4   Brewington, 2-4, 8, 12.

OTHER WORDS AND EXPRESSIONS

*W*hen you receive a *windfall*, do you think of a huge tree being toppled by the wind? Or when you *bury the hatchet* with an opponent, do you actually see the end of the hatchet sticking out of the ground as colonial men and women did? Probably not. Many of our most colorful expressions and words, though, had their origins in the life and times of the colonists, and understanding their early usage enriches our appreciation of their meanings today.

Ain't

Then

*I*n colonial days, **ain't** was an acceptable contraction of *am not*. It had started as *an't* in England and came to the American shores as such but soon became *ain't* on both sides of the Atlantic. It was used by gentlemen and scholars alike. When people started carelessly using *ain't* to mean "is not," "are not," "has not," and "have not," the arbiters of correct speech relegated *ain't* to the ranks of socially unacceptable words. Soon it was disdained by all but a few English gentry and some Georgian and Carolinian aristocrats, some of whose descendants (along with the descendants of their ancestors' slaves) still retain many of the early usages and patterns of speech.[1]

Now

Ain't today is considered a socially unacceptable, but widely used, contraction of *am not*.

An axe to grind
————————————————————Then

An old axe much in need of a grinding.

Perhaps the fact that this phrase has been erroneously attributed to Ben Franklin arises from Franklin's role as the originator of so many other well-known phrases. The apocryphal story has it that Franklin was asked by a visitor, who professed to admire his father's grindstone, how the thing worked. As young Ben demonstrated, the man put his axe up to the grindstone and had it sharpened at the expense of Ben's energy and with no recompense. Ben thus had **an axe to grind** with the fellow.

The story of someone flattering a young boy into sharpening his axe was not published until the early 1800s, although the expression to *have an axe to grind* may well have been used before that time.

Now————————————————————

To have **an axe to grind** means to harbor a grudge or to have suffered a wrong that a person intends to have redressed.

Bee
————————————————————Then

In colonial days, **bees**, sometimes called frolics or entertainments, were gatherings at which neighbors came together to share in completing a task. There were sewing bees, husking bees, raising (house) bees, and apple-paring bees. There were timber or log rollings, stone pullings, and sheep shearings. These gatherings combined the functional with the social, allowing the participants a break from their everyday work. After the project was completed, there were often refreshments, socializing, games, and dancing.

In 1767, Mr. Ames of Dedham described a corn husking, for what he hoped was posterity:

> *Possibly this leafe may last a Century and fall into the hands*
> *of some inquisitive Person for whose Entertainm't I will*
> *inform him that now there is a Custom amongst us of making*
> *an Entertainm't at husking of Indian Corn whereto all the*
> *neighboring Swains are invited and after the Corn is finished*
> *they like the Hottentots give three Cheers or huzza's but cannot*
> *carry in the husks without a Rhum bottle; they feign great*
> *Exertion but do nothing till Rhum enlivens them, when all is*
> *done in a trice, then after a hearty Meal about 10 at Night they*
> *go to their pastimes.*[2]

Now

A **bee** is still a gathering at which people both socialize and work, and often compete. Today it is typically associated with the spelling bee where youngsters meet in competition to determine the best speller in the school, state, or country.

Bundling

Then

For many, **bundling**—the lying together of a courting couple fully or partially clothed (sometimes separated by a length of board between them) —was an accepted custom. In an age when winters were fiercely cold and wood for fire expensive, bundling was deemed a reasonable economy. Wrote one poet:

> *Since in a bed a man and maid,*
> *May bundle and be chaste,*
> *It does no good to burn out wood,*
> *It is a needless waste.*[3]

Not every maid was able to remain chaste, it appears:

> *Cate, Nance and Sue proved just and true,*
> *Tho' bundling did practise;*

> But Ruth beguil'd and proved with child,
> Who bundling did despise.[4]

Most early homes were small and crowded, so the bundling couple was never truly alone. Nevertheless, for added peace of mind, the colonists invented ingenious devices to ensure the young woman's chastity. These included bundling stockings which bound her legs and feet together, and a bundling apron which wrapped securely around her from waist to feet. An early ballad sang:

> But she is modest, also chaste
> While only bare from neck to waist,
> And he of boasted freedom sings,
> Of all above her apron strings.[5]

They also devised a courting stick – a hollowed out length of wood through which the couple could whisper of their love without being overheard by family members in the room with them.[6]

At times, bundling was practiced as a way to accommodate an overnight guest when beds were scarce—the guest sharing a bed with the wife or daughter of the house. Thomas Anburey records this of his stop in 1777 at a "small log-hut" near Williamstown.

> I was convinced in how innocent a view the Americans look upon that indelicate custom they call bundling; though they have remarkable good feather beds, and are extremely neat and clean, still I preferred my hard mattrass, as being accustomed to it; this evening, however, owing to the badness of the roads, and weakness of my mare, my servant had not arrived with my baggage, at the time for retiring to rest; there being only two beds in the house, I enquired which I was to sleep in, when the old woman replied, "Mr. Ensign," … "Our Jonathan and I will sleep in this, and our Jemima and you shall sleep in that." I was much astonished at such a proposal, and offered to sit up all night, when Jonathan immediately replied, "Oh, la! Mr. Ensign, you won't be the first man our Jemima has bundled with, will it Jemima?" when little Jemima, who, by the bye, was a very pretty black-eyed girl, of about 16 or 17, archly replied, "No, Father, by many, but it will be with the first Britainer," (the name they give to Englishmen.) In this dilemma, what could I do—the smiling invitation of pretty Jemima—the eye, the lip, the—Lord ha' mercy, where am I going to? But wherever I may be going to now,

I did not go to bundle with her … . Suppose how great the test of virtue must be, or how cold the American constitution, when this unaccountable custom is in hospitable repute, and perpetual practice. [7]

Bundling was on the wane by the late 1700s.

Now

Bundling is the gathering into one pile or collection any number of objects (or perhaps, as in colonial days, teenagers).

Bury the hatchet

Then

Burying the hatchet was a physical act carried out by New England Native Americans to mark the end of hostilities. Conflicts very well may have begun with the taking up of the hatchet, but it was preferable to end them by

Replica of hatchet used by colonial militia. From a private collection.

burying the weapon in the ground rather than in the opponent's scull. There were similar phrases, like "bury the tomahawk" or "bury the axe." Samuel Sewell recorded in 1680:

Meeting with the Sachem [an Indian chief] they came to an agreement and buried two axes in the ground, which ceremony to them is more significant and binding than all the Articles of Peace the hatchet being the principal weapon. [8]

Many New Englanders serving in the colonial militia equipped themselves with hatchets in addition to muskets, bayonets, and swords.

Now

To **bury the hatchet** still means to make peace between enemies.

Buxom

Then

To the colonists, a person—man or woman—who was **buxom** was lively, brisk, obedient, or submissive. Even drink personified took on the quality of "bucksome" in this poem:

> To the Tavern lets away!
> There have I a Mistress got,
> Cloystered in a Pottle Pot;
> Plump and bounding, soft and fair,
> Bucksome, sweet and debonair,
> And they call her Sack my Dear![9]

Now

Buxom is a term describing a well-endowed woman.

Clip

Then

Clip was the term used for illicitly shaving or cutting the edges off of colonial silver or gold coins. Massachusetts established a mint in the early 1650s to make silver coins, but these coins almost immediately had to be redesigned since the pattern on their face left too much empty surface around the edges that pilferers could clip. The clipper over time would amass enough of the precious metal to recast into jewelry or silverware, thereby easily hiding his theft. A Boston newspaper in 1705, published the general courts' ruling "Prohibiting the Importation of any clipt Money."[10]

> The G—— ——t, says a correspondent, do the same by the people in general as the clippers and coiners do by the current specie, viz.
> They clip us of our privileges,
> Diminish our bodies by starving us,
> Sweat us with taxes and imposts,
> Cut us to pieces in St. George's Fields, Boston, &c.
> Debase us by ill examples,
> Render us light by an iniquitous management of the Scales of Justice,
> Weigh us in a false medium, by using dead weights against us, such as placemen pensioners. &c.
> And lastly, stamp us with opprobrious epithets, such as, Scum of the earth, Dregs of the people, &c.

From the Boston Evening Post, *November 15, 1773.*

Now

Clip is a slang word for steal. A clip joint is a public restaurant, bar, or nightclub that overcharges, thereby cheating its customers.

Curious
—Then

*I*n addition to meaning eager to know, **curious** to New Englanders meant excellent or peculiarly excellent. Anna Winslow wrote in her diary:

> Some time since I exchang'd a piece of patchwork, which had been wrought in my leisure intervals, with Miss Peggy Phillips, my schoolmate, for a pair of curious lace mitts with blue flaps which I shall send, with a yard of white ribbin edg'd with green to Miss Nancy Macky for a present.[11]

> Leather, IndiaHandkerchiefs, the greateſt variety of moſt curious Pictures, pick & chuſe for 6d & 12d a Piece —Likewiſe a curious parcel of Haberdaſhery Articles, Men's Buff-leather Gloves,

Excerpt from an ad offering curious pictures and curious parcel of Haberdashery Articles, the Boston Evening Post, *November 15, 1773.*

Now

Curious, in describing a person, means desirous of learning and investigating. In describing a thing, it means distinct in an unusual way.

Dead as a doornail
—Then

*N*ails in colonial days were hand wrought and valuable; they would have been reused whenever possible. Nails were used to stabilize the panels of a door to keep the panels from going aslant. Frequently, when a nail protruded through the wood to the other side, the pointed end would be hammered flat, thus clinching the nail to give better stability to the door while at the same time making the nail unusable for any other purpose—thus, **dead as a doornail.**

Now

Dead as a doornail today means totally inanimate, completely without life or use.

Dicker
Then

*T*he colonists used the term **dicker** in the same way that they had been accustomed to in England. There, the term *dicer* (derived from the Latin word *decuria* meaning ten of something, usually ten hides) referred to the ten hides that the Romans used as their bartering unit with the Anglo-Saxons. The frontier colonists in turn applied the term to their negotiations with the Indians for fur skins.

Now

Today, to **dicker** means to bargain or negotiate a price for something.

Fly off the Handle
Then

An axe head attached to its wooden handle.

*T*he hammer, the hatchet, the axe and other such tools consisted of the head with a hole through which the wooden handle was driven. When the wood dried out, it no longer held the head securely in place. At times, the loose head would **fly off the handle**. Whoever was hit by the missile might well have been tempted to *fly off the handle* himself.

Now————————————————————————

To **fly off the handle** means to lose control and get violently, rashly angry.

Flying machine
————————————————————————*Then*

AMERICAN STAGE-COACH OF 1795, FROM "WELD'S TRAVELS." (PROBABLY SIMILAR IN FORM TO THOSE OF THE LATER COLONIAL PERIOD.)

American stagecoach of 1795 from "Weld's Travels."

The **flying machine** was the name given to a stagecoach known to be particularly fast. A trip from Boston to New York in the early 1700s could take up to seven days, depending on the condition of the roads and the weather. A fast-moving coach that promised to make the trip in fewer days would indeed seem as though it were flying.

An English visitor noted:

> Seven and one-half miles per hour from Boston to Providence,
> I record as being considerably the quickest rate of travelling met
> with anywhere in America.[12]

Slow or fast, though, the trip was far from easy, as one weary traveler lamented:

> The carriages were old and shackling, and much of the harness
> made of ropes. One pair of horses carried the stage eighteen
> miles. We generally reached our resting place for the night, if
> no accident intervened, at ten o'clock, and after a frugal supper
> went to bed with a notice that we should be called at three the
> next morning, which generally proved to be half-past two. Then,
> whether it snowed or rained, the traveller must rise and make
> ready by the help of a horn-lantern and a farthing candle, and
> proceed on his way over bad roads, sometimes with a driver
> showing no doubtful symptoms of drunkenness, which good-
> hearted passengers never fail to improve at every stopping place

> *by urging upon him another glass of toddy. Thus we travelled,*
> *eighteen miles a stage, sometimes obliged to get out and help the*
> *coachman lift the coach out of a quagmire or rut, and arrived at*
> *New York after a week's hard travelling, wondering at the ease as*
> *well as expedition of our journey.*[13]

Travelers had few options other than the stagecoach unless they wanted to go by foot, by horseback, or by water. The roads, having started as Indian trails or footpaths, were narrow, rutted, muddy morasses in spring and solid, frozen washboards in winter. In 1704, Sarah Knight, having crossed a hazardous river "knowing that I must either Venture my fate of drowning, or be left like ye children in the wood," found still more difficulty in "Travailing",

> *The way being very narrow, and on each side the Trees and*
> *bushes gave us very unpleasant welcomes wth their Branches and*
> *bow's, wch wee could not avoid … . Now Returned my distressed*
> *aprehensions of the place where I was: the dolesome woods,*
> *my Company next to none, Going I knew not whither, and*
> *encompassed wth Terrifying darkness.*[14]

Not until after the Revolution did private companies undertake to improve the roads, making them smoother, wider, straighter, and better drained, often shortening the travel time between towns by half. The turnpikes that they built were toll roads from which they hoped to reap a large profit, but the cost of upkeep and the ingenuity of travelers in avoiding the tolls thwarted their hopes. One poet penned:

> *The road, the road, the turnpike road*
> *The hard, the brown, the smooth, the broad*
> *Without a mark, without a bend*
> *Horses 'gainst horses on it contend.*
> *Men laugh at gates, they bilk the tolls*
> *Or stop and pay like honest souls … .*[15]

Now

Flying machine is now a term for the early prototypes of airplanes or dirigibles or for any experimental machine designed to fly.

Football

————————————————————————————————*Then*

*I*n colonial times, a game known as **football** or "the Boston game" developed as a variation of the folk game brought over from England, the objective being to kick a ball across a goal line. The playing of unregulated football games on town streets was frowned upon and considered a nuisance by the Puritans. Having already, in 1646, outlawed shuffleboard and bowling, the General Court passed an ordinance against football in 1657:

> *Forasmuch as sundry complaints are made that several persons*
> *have received hurt by boys and young men playing at football*
> *in the streets, these therefore are to enjoin that none be found at*
> *that game in any of the streets, lanes or enclosures of this town*
> *under the penalty of twenty shillings for every such offence.*[16]

In the eighteenth century, the game found its way onto college campuses, although not till the end of the 1700s were the various school rules finally standardized leading toward the game as we know it today.[17]

Now————————————————————————————————

Football is the game, very popular in the United States, that scarce needs description, if the size of the audience annually watching the Super Bowl is anything to go by.

Frolic

————————————————————————————————*Then*

A **frolic**, like a bee, was a planned event that saw friends and neighbors gather together to accomplish a task or to socialize. In 1737, a minister commented, perhaps with disapproval:

> *It was their manner to frequently get together in conventions of*
> *both sexes for mirth and jollity which they called frolics.* [18]

Young people especially flocked to the frolics and bees, corn huskings, sheep shearings, where they could show off their skills, strengths, and industry and afterwards court their potential mates at the dancing and play that followed. This combination of work and courtship satisfied the community's need to ensure that time was well spent while it allowed for courting in an acceptable manner.

Turtle frolics were especially popular, with the turtles provided by ships' captains returning with the coveted prizes from the West Indies. The turtles were cooked, eaten, and washed down with copious amounts of liquor. People at all levels of society enjoyed these outings. Manasseh Cutler, minister and lawmaker in Providence, Rhode Island, bemoaned:

> *This morning I received a polite invitation from Governor Bowen*
> *in the name of a large company to join them in a Turtle Frolic*
> *about six miles out of town. Mr. Hitchcock and other clergymen*
> *of the town were of the party but much against my inclination I*
> *was obliged to excuse myself.* [19]

Quilting frolics were common among women, providing them with an opportunity for mutual help as well as companionship. Other frolics, it appears from this gentleman's diary entry, were planned purely for social purposes:

> *Edward Emerson was twenty one years old he made an*
> *entertainment for the young gentlemen and Ladies it was*
> *exceeding bad travailing notwithstanding the young Ladies were*
> *so much engaged on the Frollic that they went Knee Deep in*
> *Snow water to honor Mr. Emerson and see and get sweethearts.* [20]

Now

To **frolic** is to have a lively, carefree time. It's not commonly used as a noun any more.

Hearse
Then

To the colonists, a **hearse** was a decorated wooden structure erected over the grave of a notable person. It was also a platform on which a coffin rested surrounded by candles. Since there were no eulogies and no spoken words at early Puritan funerals—the Puritans wishing not to "confirm the popish error that prayer is to be used for the dead or over the dead"[21] —friends and relatives placed their own private messages and verses on the hearse. Reading the following epitaph that Governor Thomas Dudley wrote before his own death in 1653, we might surmise that abstaining from reading such poems aloud was not a bad practice:

> *Dim eyes, deaf ears, cold stomach show*
> *My dissolution is in view;*
> *Eleven times seven near lived have I,*
> *And now God calls, I willing die;*
> *My shuttle's shot, my race is run,*
> *My sun is set, my deed is done;*
> *My span is measure'd, tale is told,*
> *My flower is faded and grown old,*
> *My dream is vanish'd, shadow's fled,*
> *My soul with Christ, my body dead;*
> *Farewell dear wife, children and friends,*
> *Hate heresy, make blessed ends;*
> *Bear poverty, live with good men,*
> *So shall we meet with joy again.*
> *Let men of God in courts and churches watch*
> *O'er such as do a toleration hatch;*
> *Lest that ill egg bring forth a cockatrice,*
> *To prison all with heresy and vice.*
> *If men be left, and other wise combine*
> *My epitaph's, I dy'd no libertine.*[22]

Governor Dudley and his fellow Puritans would brook no huggermugger, their term for secrecy or privacy, "lest that ill egg bring forth a cockatrice," the cockatrice being an evil mythical creature with killing glance and poisonous breath.

The Puritans had a melancholy view of life and a dread of death, both drawn from their Calvinist faith. Social historian David Hackett Fischer wrote:

> *The fabled "Five Points" of New England's Calvinist orthodoxy insisted that the natural condition of humanity was total depravity, that salvation was beyond mortal striving, that grace was predestined only*

A gravestone, dated 1744, showing typical early carvings, from the old Lexington burying ground.

*for a few, that most mortals were condemned to suffer eternal
damnation, and no earthly effort could save them.*[23]

No wonder they feared death! Best to get the dead into the ground quickly
and let heaven decide whether the deceased was graced or damned. That
did not mean, though, that the death went uncelebrated in its fashion. A
funeral became an occasion to show off one's finest clothing and to give and
receive expensive mourning gifts, usually rings or gloves. In addition, large
quantities of rum, whiskey, and cider were served along with punch made
with lemons, spices, and sugar. Towns even gave paupers a barrel of cider or
a few gallons of rum, and the church would often pay the bill for liquor at
the funeral of a minister.

Nathaniel Hawthorne mused that funerals

*were the only class of scenes, so far as my investigation has
taught me, in which our ancestors were wont to steep their tough
old hearts in wine and strong drink and indulge in an outbreak
of grisly jollity. Look back through all the social customs of New
England in the first century of her existence and ... find one
occasion other than
a funeral feast where
jollity was sanctioned
by universal practice
... . New England
must have been a
dismal abode for
the man of pleasure
when the only
boon-companion was
Death.*[24]

Query, Whether it is best at present to discoun-
tenance the extravagance in dress, or be content
to pay for every thing so much more than is necessary for any other purpose than for the support
of that vanity which tends to idleness and disso-
luteness of manners.

And whereas very great savings were made by
not going into extravagant mourning at the funeral of our relations, and never a time more necessary than the present for œconomy :

Questioning the extravagance of funerals, from the Boston
Gazette and Country Journal, *August 26, 1782.*

Now

A **hearse** today is a special carriage or car used to transport a coffin to the
church or cemetery.

Holdfast
————————————————————————————*Then*

A **holdfast,** also called a *dog*, was a bench tool hand forged by the local blacksmith, used to hold a plank of wood that the colonial carpenter (house builders) or cabinetmaker (called *joiner* until the 1700s) was working on. A holdfast consisted of a kind of jam hook that went into the wood at an angle to hold it securely. Carpenters' and cabinetmakers' helpers, journeymen (paid workers), and apprentices (unpaid young people who received room and board, education, and training for a set period) were taught to use the tools and were allowed to perform the less skilled parts of the craft.

> JUST COME TO HAND,
> *A* ND to be Sold, at the Store of Penuel Bowen, opposite the Golden Ball, a small parcel of new and useful Goods, viz. Locks, Hinges, Bolts, Spikes, Hoes, Coopers and Joiners Tools, broad Axes, gauging Rods, London Porter, Glocester Cheese, Olives, Ca-

Tools for sale in the Independent Chronicle and Universal Advertiser, *August 7, 1777.*

Now————————————————————————————

A **holdfast** is a device or instrument designed to fasten something securely.

Milestone
————————————————————————————*Then*

S ingle **milestones** had been set in place by a few New England towns to inform travelers of the distance along that particular road or path to the next town; but it was Ben Franklin, with his inventiveness and, what would come to be called "Yankee," ingenuity, who put them to good commercial use. When, in 1753, Benjamin Franklin was appointed associate postmaster for the Royal Post in the colonies, he personally inspected all of the major post roads in the country to figure out how best to end the frequent arguments between customers and clerks over the actual mileage their mail traveled. Distance as well as weight determined the postage charged for a piece of mail, and Franklin knew that unless the miles were accurately measured, the arguments would continue indefinitely. He invented an odometer, a fifth wheel with a known circumference, which he attached to the hub of his carriage. By counting rotations of this wheel, he was able to measure and have the workers who came after him mark measured intervals with milestones. From then on, the post riders could accurately measure the distance they had carried a letter or almanac or newspaper between towns along the three major post roads that went, by different routes, from Boston to New York and beyond.

Milestone along the Post Road in Marlborough c 1770.

In addition to this major improvement, Franklin instituted weekly deliveries (up from two a winter), efficient bookkeeping, and additional post boys. Of one particularly effective improvement, he wrote:

> By making the Mails travel by Night as well as by Day, Letters may be sent and answers received in four Days, which before took a fortnight.[25]

Benjamin Franklin is also credited with creating the word *mileage* in 1757, when he proposed that representatives from the various colonies be compensated for the distance they would travel to and from a proposed, and in his opinion much desired, colonial council.

Now

A **milestone** is a turning point or important moment in a timeframe (a person's life, an event, or a company goal reached). It also retains its colonial meaning, with stone markers (some of the first ones are still in place today) marking the miles along the Boston Post Roads.

Pen

Then

*I*n colonial days, a quill **pen** was fashioned from the hollow shaft of a large feather of a goose, turkey, or swan. The colonists carefully pointed and split the end of the quill with a pen or quill knife. The two resulting nibs, when dipped into ink, turned the feather into a fine writing instrument.

Quill pens.

For the colonists, letter writing was essential as the only means of communicating with people to whom they could not talk in person. When John Adams prepared to sail to France in 1778 to negotiate for French money and manpower to aid the Patriots in the Revolutionary War, he took on board with him, among other things (including a case of rum), "1/4 hundred Quills" along with ink, sealing wax, and account books.[26]

The ability to write could be put to less noble purposes as well, as this notice illustrates:

> *Thomas Read … Ran-away from the Subscriber … . is a Jeweller, and Motto-Ring Engraver, and is a very artful talkative pert Fellow: —can write pretty well, and has doubtless help'd himself to a Discharge, Pass, or any other Writing to deceive, and suit his Purpose.*[27]

Paper and writing implements were highly valued. Paper, largely imported from England, was made from cloth rags that were ground to a pulp, mixed with water, and spread on a mesh frame to form sheets—a complicated, labor-intensive process. Judge Sewell in 1717 thought it generous to give a potential marriage candidate "A Quire of Paper, a good Leathern Ink Horn, a stick of Sealing Wax and 200 Wafers [ink] in a little Box."[28] (She must already have had the quill pens.)

Now

Today's **pen** is a metal or plastic writing instrument used to write with ink.

Penknife

A **penknife** was the small sharp knife used to point and cut the split in the barrel of a quill. In 1765, the company of Rivington and Miller in Boston informed "their Customers and others" that they had a "fine Assortment of Penknives, 2, 3 & 4 Blades, made by the best hands in England ... ."[29]

Jackknives were also available, and every boy yearned to own one of these small versatile knives. In an age when personal possessions, especially toys, were scarce and expensive, a boy could use a jackknife to whittle all sorts of entertaining and useful things, as the Reverend Pierpont described:

> *The Yankee boy before he's sent to school*
> *Well knows the mysteries of that magic tool –*
> *The pocket-knife. To that his wistful eye*
> *Turns, while he hears his mother's lullaby.*
> *And in the education of the lad,*
> *No little part that implement hath had.*
> *His pocket-knife to the young whittler brings*
> *A growing knowledge of material things,*
> *Projectiles, music, and the sculptor's art.*
> *His chestnut whistle, and his shingle dart,*
> *His elder pop-gun with its hickory rod,*
> *Its sharp explosion and rebounding wad,*
> *His corn-stalk fiddle, and the deeper tone*
> *That murmurs from his pumpkin-leaf trombone*
> *Conspire to teach the boy. To these succeed*
> *His bow, his arrow of a feathered reed,*
> *His windmill raised the passing breeze to win,*
> *His water-wheel that turns upon a pin.*
> *Thus by his genius and his jack-knife driven*
> *Ere long he'll solve you any problem given;*
> *Cut a canal or build a floating dock:*
> *Make anything in short for sea or shore,*
> *From a child's rattle to a seventy-four.*
> *Make it, said I—ay, when he undertakes it,*
> *He'll make the thing and make the thing that makes it.*[30]

Now—————————————————————————

A **penknife** is the name of any small knife easily carried in a pocket.

Podunk
————————————————————————*Then*

*T*o the colonists, the term **Podunk** referred to poor neighborhoods or villages where housing was mean and rundown and where inhabitants scratched out a meager living from the poor soil. The terms *hardscrabble* or *two-penny parish* were also used to describe such places.[31] Podunk was also a place name used by Indians in Massachusetts and Connecticut and is still the name of towns in Vermont and Connecticut.

Now—————————————————————————

Podunk conjures up the image of a small, isolated, backwater town inhabited by boors and bumpkins.

Pull the wool over one's eyes
————————————————————————*Then*

*I*n the days when men wore wigs, one person could tip a wig (frequently made of wool) over the wearer's eyes thereby momentarily blinding him to what was happening around him.

In the 1700s, wigs were worn nearly universally in New England. Men of all ranks—gentlemen, yeomen, mechanics, sailors, soldiers, boys, servants, prisoners—

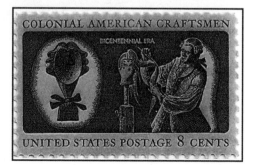

all wore them. One notice in the *Boston News-Letter*, April 21/28, 1712, advertised for help finding a runaway:

> *Sailor – … aged about 19 years, a tall man, pretty much pock broken, short black Hair, a black Wigg: …* [32]

Another in August 1716 advertising for a runaway periwig maker:

> *Ran away … a North Britain Man Servant, named David Dowie, a Perriwig-maker, of middle Stature, fresh Colour, aged about 24 Years, wears a Perriwig, a Cinamon coloured Coat, Round to'd Shoes.* [33]

There was a large assortment of wigs to choose from as this notice by a wig maker in 1753 suggests:

> *Made by James Mitchell, at his Shop in King-street … After the best and newest Fashion: Tye Wiggs, full bottom Wiggs, Brigadiers, Spencers, Cues, Bag Wiggs, Albemarles, Scratches, cut and curl'd Wiggs …* [34]

The bigger the wig, the more important the wearer; thus the expression "bigwig."

In 1717, Judge Samuel Sewell, recently widowed, was wooing a widow whom he hoped to marry until, that is, she proposed that he wear a wig. Hating those "horrid Bushes of Vanity," he wrote her back:

> *As to a Periwigg my best and Greatest Friend begun to find me with Hair before I was born and has continued to do so ever since and I could not find it in my heart to go to another.* [35]

She was not moved by this argument and ended their relationship. To console himself, he confided in his diary that she had not had on "Clean Linen" and that "Her dress was not so clean as sometimes it had been," and he moved on to court another. [36] No one would **pull the wool over his eyes**.

In colonial days, the Free Masons **pulled wool scarves over the eyes** of their initiates to blindfold them as part of the initiation ceremony.

Now

To **pull the wool over one's eyes** means to fool someone, to hoodwink or deceive him.

Resent

————————————————————————————————*Then*

Resent meant to accept something with great pleasure or to feel deeply. The Puritan Reverend Mr. Winthrop was eager to have his wife emigrate from England to Boston to join him in 1632, but he was unable to convince her to leave the comforts of her home for this unknown land. He decided to travel back to England to fetch her, bearing three gifts: a "*brass* counter, a *silver* crown, and a *gold* jacobus [a valuable English coin], all severally wrapped up." He was counseled to give her first the brass counter and,

> *if she received it with any shew of discontent, he should then take*
> *no notice of her; but if she gratefully **resented** that small thing*
> *for the sake of the hand it came from, he should then go on to*
> *deliver the silver and so the gold, but withal assure her that such*
> *would be the dispensations to her and the good people of New*
> *England.*[37]

It was hardly any wonder that Mrs. Winthrop might hesitate to come to a strange and harsh new land, but come she did.

Now————————————————————————————————

Resent means to feel indignant or bitter about an act or statement. Mrs. Winthrop may well have resented her husband, in today's meaning of the word, for bringing her to New England, but we will never know.

Sad

————————————————————————————————*Then*

Sad had two meanings in addition to being downcast. One referred to a range of sad, subdued colors widely favored by the colonists including, according to a 1638 list, "liver color, de Boys, tawney, russet, purple, French green, ginger-lyne, deer colour, orange,"[38] as well as somber greens, flax, puce, and other such hues.

Madam Knight wrote in her diary in 1704 of her stay at an inn on the road:

> *I pray'd Miss to shew me where I must Lodg. Shee conducted me*
> *to a parlour in a little back Lento, wch was almost filled wth the*

> *bedstead, wch was so high that I was forced to climb on a chair to*
> *gitt up to ye wretched bed that lay on it, on wch having Strecht my*
> *tired Limbs, and lay'd my head on a Sad-colour'd pillow, I began*
> *to think on the transactions of ye past day.*[39]

Sad was also used in its older English sense of "grave, serious, wise, discreet, settled, steadfast and firm."[40] Colonists associated these commendable qualities of intelligence and trustworthiness with age as reflected in John Adams's statement:

> *None were fit for Legislators and magistrates but 'sad men'*
> *… aged men who had been tossed and buffeted by the*
> *vicissitudes of Life, forced upon profound reflection by grief and*
> *disappointments, and taught to command their passions.*[41]

Now

Sad retains only one of the colonial meanings, the one describing an emotional state characterized by unhappiness, depression, or sorrow.

Slang
Then

The word **slang** was first used in the colonies in its combined form, *slang-whanger,* to mean a newspaper writer. Writing in 1816 of what he termed "Americanisms," John Pickering made note of "the favourite compound term 'slang-whanger' for a newspaper-writer." He went on to add that it was also the term for:

> *A noisy talker, who makes use of that sort of political or other*
> *cant, which amuses the rabble, and is called by the vulgar name*
> *of* slang. *It is hardly necessary to add, that this term (as well*
> *as* slang-whanger) *is never admitted into the higher kinds of*
> *writing; but, like other cant words, is confined to that familiar*
> *style, which is allowed only in works of humour.*[42]

Now——————————————————————————

Slang is the term for nonconventional, colloquial words and phrases used informally and in common speech but not in formal writing.

Smug

————————————————————————*Then*

When a colonial gentleman was called **smug**, he was being complimented for his smart, neat appearance. A man gotten up smugly was well and handsomely dressed.

Now—————————————————

Smug means self-righteous, self-satisfied, and complacent. (It is not a compliment.)

A colonial revival (late 1800s) depiction of smugly dressed colonists from an illustration entitled Toasting the Bride.

Talk turkey

————————————————————————*Then*

The story goes that a colonial hunter and an Indian went together in search of game. Before they left, they had agreed to split the take evenly. At the end of their hunt, they had crows and turkeys in their bag. The colonist started to divide the booty: a crow for the Indian, a turkey for the colonist, a crow for the Indian, a turkey for the colonist. Finally the Indian confronted him with these words, "You **talk all turkey** for you. Only talk crow for Indian."[43] The time had come for the two to have a serious discussion!

Now——————————————————————————

To **talk turkey** means to talk about the important matters, the meaningful business.

Tandem
——————————————————————Then

*I*n the 1700s, a **tandem** was a two-wheeled buggy or chaise drawn by two horses harnessed one in front of the other. Other forms of transportation were mentioned by John Adams in 1774 when he was deciding how to travel from Boston to Philadelphia. First he couldn't make up his mind whether to have his new suit of clothes made in Boston or in Philadelphia; then he continued, "nor do I know how I shall go—whether on Horse back, in a Curricle, a Phaeton, or altogether in a Stage Coach I know not."[44] The curricle and phaeton were both small, fast, light carriages much like the tandem. Another "clumsy, ill contrived covered carriage" was called a babyhutt or a booby-hutch. Anna Winslow says of her aunt:

Sketch of a phaeton.

> *If she had wanted much to have seen me, she might have sent either one of her chaises, her chariot, or her babyhutt, one of which I see going by the door almost every day.*[45]

Now——————————————————————

Today, **tandem** signifies one thing coming before the other, as in two seats on a tandem bicycle, one in front of the other. The phrase *in tandem* means the same thing: having one object, person, or event arranged in front of or before another.

Tarry
——————————————————————Then

*T*o **tarry** was a courting custom that remained even after bundling was no longer practiced. The British soldier Thomas Anburey, who spent time in Boston as a lightly-guarded prisoner of war in the 1770s, observed:

> *Apropos, as to that custom [bundling], along the sea coast, by a continual intercourse among Europeans, it is in some measure*

abolished; but they still retain one something similar, which is termed tarrying.

When a young man is enamoured of a woman, and wishes to marry her, he proposes the affair to her parents, (without whose consent no marriage, in this colony, can take place) if they have no objection, he is allowed to tarry with her one night, in order to make his court. At the usual time, the old couple retire to bed, leaving the young ones to settle matters as they can, who, having sat up as long as they think proper, get into bed together also, but without putting off their under garments, to prevent scandal. If the parties agree, it is all very well, and the banns are published, and they married [sic] without delay; if not, they part, and possibly never see each other again, unless, which is an accident that seldom happens, the forsaken fair proves pregnant, in which case the man, unless he absconds, is obliged to marry her, on pain of excommunication.[46]

Now

Tarry means to dawdle, to linger or loiter—that is to stay longer in one place than seems normal, usually with the subtext of a good reason for delay. In this respect, the connection to the colonial usage seems apparent.

The third degree
Then

*I*n order for a colonial Free Mason to pass from one level of proficiency to the next in the Masonic order, he was required to pass a test. Starting with the entered apprentice degree, the aspirant would work to do what was required to achieve the Second Degree called the fellow craft degree, and finally to pass the extremely rigorous test for the **Third Degree** to reach the highest level of Masonry, Master Mason.

Many of the leaders of the Massachusetts Patriots were active Masons. They found in the Masonic Creed of "enlightened Christianity, fraternity, harmony, reason, and community service"[47] a fitting formula for their lives. Paul Revere, John Hancock, and Joseph Warren—all three instrumental in mobilizing resistance to the British—were Masons. They helped to organize the raid on the English tea ships and the destruction of the tea in Boston harbor (not called the Tea Party until the 1830s), meeting at the Green Dragon Tavern, an elegant Boston establishment that the Masons had bought to be their Masonic Hall. Benjamin Franklin and George Washington were among many Masons who played critical roles in securing America's independence.

Now

In addition to still being the final test to become a Master Mason, **the third degree** also connotes an intensive grilling by an interrogator or police investigator.

Torpedo
Then

*I*n colonial days, a **torpedo** was a flat, circular-bodied, ray-like fish with a tapering tail; it was also known as an electric ray because it was capable of emitting from its body a strong electrical current that caused a severe shock to a person who came in contact with it. Dead, the fish was perfectly edible. Colonists also used the expression *to torpedo*, meaning to stun or make numb.

Deck Nails down to 4d,— Fish Hooks of different sorts, from large Cod Hooks down to Trout Hooks,—Cod Lines,—St. Peter's Lines, &c.—Mackrel dit,—WindowGlafs, 7 by 9, and 8 by 10— And a Number of other Articles,—— ☞ LUMBER, FISH or WEST INDIA GOODS, will be re-ceiv'd in Payment for any of the above Goods.   Portfmouth, June 9, 1772.

Advertisement for fish hooks and lines in the New Hampshire Gazette and Historical Chronicle, *June 11, 1773.*

The colonists fished in fresh water for alewife, bass, shad, smelts, sun fish, perch, dace, shiner, trout, pickerel, horned pout, suckers, common eel, lamprey eel, and stone suckers. They fished in the Atlantic for cod, mackerel, halibut, herring, salmon, sturgeon, haddock, fluke, sea flounder, dory, turbot, and whales, to name only some. They also harvested clams, mussels, cockles, and lobsters. Lobsters were so abundant, even washing up onto shore in piles, and so large, sometimes weighing over forty pounds, that they were used as bait, as fertilizer, and as food for pigs, cattle, prisoners, and the poor. It is said that some indentured servants had written into their contract the stipulation that they would be made to eat lobster (and salmon, also abundant in streams and ocean) no more than two or three times a week.

Now

A **torpedo** is a cylindrical, explosives-charged, self-propelled metal tube that, when launched from a ship, submarine, or plane, travels underwater until it explodes on impact with or near an intended target. Sailors call these torpedoes *fish*—perhaps an unknowing bow to the colonial meaning.

The British Angler, *1740.*

Windfall

Then

*I*n the colonial era, the English government reserved the largest pine trees of the colonies' virgin forests for use by the Crown to make masts for the king's ships. It was illegal for the colonists to cut down trees inscribed with the royal broad-arrow mark. The colonists could use only those trees felled by the wind; hence the word **windfall** for this unanticipated but much desired bounty.

Now

A **windfall** refers to any unexpected but very welcome gain, such as the receipt of a bonus at work or an inheritance. It also refers to fruit that the wind shakes loose from the trees.

OTHER WORDS AND EXPRESSIONS

Chapter Notes:

1   Flexner, 5.

2   Earle, *Home Life,* 54.

3   Nylander, 96.

4   Ulrich and Stabler, *30.*

5   Fischer, *Albion's Seed,* 80.

6   Fischer, *Albion's Seed,* 79.

7   Anburey, *Travels,* vol. 2, 41-43

8   Morris, 100.

9   Forbes and Eastman, *Taverns and Stagecoaches,* vol. II, 10.

10   Lederer, 51.

11   *Diary of Anna Green Winslow,* 62.

12   Forbes and Eastman, *Taverns and Stagecoaches,* vol. I, 4.

13   Earle, *Stagecoach and Tavern Days,* 294.

14   Knight, 7.

15   Forbes and Eastman, *Taverns and Stagecoaches,* vol. I, 93.

16   Quoted Earle, *Customs and Fashions,* 18.

17   Fischer, *Albion's Seed,* 148-149. Fischer says, "Classical American football slowly took shape in New England during the eighteenth century as an elaborately rationalized and rule-bound version of an old English field sport."

18   Lederer, 97.

19   Earle, *Colonial Dames,* 223-224.

20   Nylander, 225.

21   Earle, *Customs and Fashions,* 364.

22   *Diary of Anna Green Winslow,* 106.

23   Fischer, *Albion's Seed,* 112.

24   Earle, *Customs and Fashions,* 370-371.

25   Jaffe, 42-43.

26   Butterfield, ed., 205.

27   Dow, *Arts and Crafts,* 71.

28   Earle, *Customs and Fashions,* 55.

29   Dow, *Arts and Crafts,* 235-236.

30   Earle, *Home Life,* 123-124.

31   Nylander, 164.

32   Dow, *Arts and Crafts,* 185

33   Dow, *Arts and Crafts,* 186.

34   Dow, *Arts and Crafts,* 291.

35   Earle, *Customs and Fashions,* 53.

36   Earle, *Customs and Fashions,* 53.

37   Earle, *Colonial Dames,* 19.

38   Fischer, *Albion's Seed,* 140.

39   Knight, 4.

40   Fischer, *Albion's Seed,* 109.

41   Fischer, *Albion's Seed,* 109.

42   Pickering, 173.

43   Morris, 555-556.

44   Butterfield, ed., 61.

45   *Diary of Anna Green Winslow,* 60.

46   Anburey, *Travels,* vol. 2, 96-98.

47   Fischer, *Paul Revere's Ride,* 19-20.

BIBLIOGRAPHY

All Sorts of Good Sufficient Cloth: Linen Making in New England 1640-1860. North Andover, MA: Merrimack Valley Textile Museum, 1980.

The American Heritage Dictionary, 2nd College Edition, 1991.

Anburey, Thomas. *Travels Through the Interior Parts of America: Eyewitness Accounts of the American Revolution.* New York: *The New York Times* and Arno Press, 1969.

Archer, Richard. *As if an Enemy's Country: The British Occupation of Boston and the Origins of Revolution.* New York: Oxford University Press, 2010.

Armentrout, Sandra S. "Eliza Wildes Bourne of Kennebunk: Professional Fancy Weaver, 1800-1820. *House and Home,* ed. Peter Benes. Boston: Boston University, 1988.

Bartlett, John Russell. *Dictionary of Americanisms: A Glossary of Words and Phrases Usually Regarded as Peculiar to the United States, 3rd ed.* Boston: Little Brown, 1860.

Bassett, Lynne Zacek. "'A Dull Business Alone': Cooperative Quilting in New England, 1750-1850." *Textiles in New England II: Four Centuries of Material Life,* ed., Peter Benes. Boston: Boston University, 1999.

Benes, Peter, ed. *American Speech: 1600 to the Present.* Boston: Boston University, 1983.

Benes, Peter, ed. *Families and Children.* Boston: Boston University, 1985.

Benes, Peter, "Itinerant Entertainers in New England and New York," 1687-1830. *Itinerancy in New England and New York.* Boston: Boston University, 1984.

Brewington, M. V. *Shipcarvers of North America.* Barre, MA: Barre Publishing Company, 1962.

Buel, Richard, Jr., and Joy Day. *The Way of Duty: A Woman and Her Family in Revolutionary America.* New York: W. W. Norton & Co., 1984.

Bushman, Richard L. *The Refinement of America: Persons, Houses, Cities.* New York: Vintage Books, 1993.

Butterfield, L. H., Marc Friedlaender, Mary Jo Kline, eds. *The Book of Abigail and John: Selected Letters of the Adams Family 1762-1784*. Cambridge, MA: Harvard University Press, 1975.

Carlo, Joyce W. *Trammels, Trenchers, & Tartlets: A Definitive Tour of the Colonial Kitchen*. Old Saybrook, CT: Peregrine Press, 1982.

Carter, Susannah. *The Frugal Colonial Housewife: A Cook's Book Wherein The Art of Dressing All Sorts of Viands With Cleanliness, Decency, and Elegance is Explained, 1772*, ed. Jean McKibbin. New York: Dolphin Books, Doubleday & Company, Inc., 1976.

Conroy, David W. *In Public Houses: Drink and the Revolution of Authority in Colonial Massachusetts*. Chapel Hill, NC: University of North Carolina Press, 1995.

Coughlin, Michelle Marchetti. *One Colonial Woman's World: The Life and Writings of Mehetabel Chandler Coit*. Amherst: University of Massachusetts Press, 2012.

Craigie, William. *The Growth of American English I*. SPE Tract No. LVI: At the Clarendon Press, 1940.

Crawford, Mary Caroline. *Little Pilgrimages Among Old New England Inns*. Boston: L. C. Page & Co., 1907.

Cummings, Abbott Lowell, ed. *Rural Household Inventories 1675-1775*. Boston: Society for the Preservation of New England Antiquities, 1964.

De Vere, Schele. *Americanisms: The English of the New World*. New York: Charles Scribner & Company, 1872.

Dexter, Elizabeth Anthony. *Colonial Women of Affairs: A Study of Women in Business and the Professions in America Before 1776*. Boston: Houghton Mifflin Company, 1924.

Diary of Anna Green Winslow: A Boston School Girl of 1771, introduction and notes by Alice Morse Earle. Bedford, MA: Applewood Books, 1894.

Dickson, Brent, and Homer Lucas. *One Town in the American Revolution:* Weston, MA: Weston Historical Society, 1976.

Dow, George Francis. *Every Day Life in the Massachusetts Bay Colony*. New York: Dover Publications, Inc., 1988.

Dow, George Francis. *The Arts and Crafts in New England, 1704-1775*. Topsfield, MA: The Wayside Press, 1927.

Dwight, Timothy. *Travels in New England and New York, Vol. I and II.* Cambridge, MA: Harvard University Press, 1969.

Earle, Alice Morse. *Child Life in Colonial Times.* Mineola, NY: Dover Publications, Inc., 2009.

Earle, Alice Morse. *Colonial Dames and Good Wives.* Boston: Houghton, Mifflin & Company Publishing Co., 1895.

Earle, Alice Morse. *Customs and Fashions in Old New England.* Rutland, VT: Charles E Tuttle, Co., 1973.

Earle, Alice Morse. *Home Life in the Colonial Days.* Stockbridge, MA: The Berkshire Traveler Press, 1898.

Earle, Alice Morse. *Stage-Coach and Tavern Days.* NY: The Macmillan Company, 1900.

Editors of the American Heritage Dictionaries. *Word Mysteries & Histories: From Quiche to Humble Pie.* Boston: Houghton Mifflin Co., 1986.

Ellery, William. *Diary of the Hon. William Ellery, of Rhode Island: October 20 to November 15, 1777. Pennsylvania Magazine of History and Biography.* The Historical Society of Pennsylvania, 1888.

Ernst, Margaret. *In A Word.* New York: Harper and Row, 1960.

Ewart, Neil. *Everyday Phrases: Their Origins and Meanings.* Poole, Dorset: Blandford Press, 1983.

Fischer, David Hackett. *Albion's Seed: Four British Folkways in America.* NY: Oxford University Press, 1989.

Fischer, David Hackett. *Paul Revere's Ride.* New York: Oxford University Press, 1994.

Flexner, Stuart Berg. *I Hear America Talking, An Illustrated Treasury of American Words and Phrases.* New York: Van Nostrand Reinhold, 1976.

Forbes, Allan, and Ralph M. Eastman. *Taverns and Stagecoaches of New England Vol. I and II.* Boston: State Street Trust Company, 1954.

Gambrill, Howard Jr., and Charles Hambrick-Stowe. *The Tavern and the Tory: The Story of the Golden Ball Tavern.* Weston, MA: 1977.

Garrett, Elisabeth Donaghy. *At Home: The American Family 1750 – 1870.* New York: Harry N. Abrams, Inc., 1990.

Gross, Robert A. *The Minutemen and Their World.* New York: Hill and Wang, 1976.

Hogan, Margaret Q., and C. James Taylor, eds. *My Dearest Friend: Letters of Abigail and John Adams.* Cambridge, MA, and London: Belknap Press of Harvard University, 2007.

Isaac Jones Family Papers. The Golden Ball Tavern Museum. Weston, MA.

Jaffe, Eric. *The King's Best Highway: The Lost History of the Boston Post Road, The Route That Made America.* New York: Scribner, 2010.

Jeans, Peter D. *Ship to Shore: A Dictionary of Everyday Words and Phrases Derived From the Sea.* Camden, ME: International Marine/McGraw-Hill, 2004.

Knight, Sarah Kemble. *The Journal of Madam Knight.* Boston: David R. Godine, 1972.

Labaree, Leonard W., ed. *Autobiography of Benjamin Franklin.* New Haven, CT: Yale University Press, 1964.

Langdon, William Chauncy. *Everyday Things in American Life, 1607-1776.* New York: Charles Scribner's Sons, 1951.

Lamson, Daniel S. *History of the Town of Weston, Massachusett, 1630-1890.* Boston: Press of Geo. H. Ellis Co., 1913.

Larkin, Jack. *The Reshaping of Everyday Life 1790-1840.* New York: Harper and Row, 1989.

Leavitt, Robert Keith. *Noah's Ark: New England Yankees and the Endless Quest.* Springfield, MA: G.C. Merriam Co, 1947.

Lederer, Richard M. Jr. *Colonial American English.* Essex, CT: A Verbatim Book, 1985.

Mack, William P., and Royal W. Connell. *Naval Ceremonies, Customs, and Traditions* (5th edition). Annapolis, MD: Naval Institute Press, 1984.

McAdam, E. L. George Milne. *Johnson's Dictionary: A Modern Selection.* New York: Pantheon Books, 1963.

McMahon, Sarah F. "A Comfortable Subsistence: The Changing Composition of Diet in Rural New England, 1620-1840," *The William and Mary Quarterly* XLII (Jan. 1985): 26-65.

Mencken, Henry Louis. *The American Language*, 4th edition. New York: Alfred A. Knopf, 1977.

Montgomery, Florence M. *Textiles in America 1650-1870: A Dictionary Based on Original Documents, Prints and Paintings, Commercial Records, American Merchants' Papers, Shopkeepers' Advertisement, and Pattern Books with Original Swatches of Cloth.* New York: W. W. Norton & Company, 1984.

Morris, William, and Mary Morris. *Morris Dictionary of Word and Phrase Origins.* New York: Harper and Row, 1977.

Nylander, Jane C. *Our Own Snug Fireside: Images of the New England Home 1760-1860.* New York: Alfred A. Knopf, 1993.

Oxford English Dictionary. Oxford, New York: Oxford University Press, 1971.

Pickering, John. *Vocabulary, or Collection of Words and Phrases Which Have Been Supposed to be Peculiar to the United States of America.* Boston: Cummings and Hilliard, 1916.

Rorabaugh, William J. *The Alcoholic Republic: An American Tradition.* New York: Oxford University Press, 1979.

Safire, William. "On Language," *The New York Times Magazine.* Nov. 14, 1993: 28.

Schaun, George, and Virginia Schaun. *Words and Phrases of Early America.* Maryland: Greenberry Publications, 1963.

Smith, Captain John, Sometimes Governor of Virginia and Admiral of New England. *Sea-man's Grammar and Dictionary, Explaining all the Difficult Terms in Navigation and the Practical Navigator and Gunner: In Two Parts.* London: Randal Taylor, 1691.

Stearns, Martha Genung. *Homespun and Blue: A Study of American Crewel Embroidery.* New York: Bonanza Books, 1963.

The First English Dictionary of Slang 1699. Oxford: The Bodleian Library, 2010.

Stuart, Nancy Rubin. *The Muse of the Revolution: The Secret Pen of Mercy Otis Warren and the Founding of a Nation.* Boston: Beacon Press, 2008.

Thoreau, Henry. D. *A Week on the Concord and Merrimac Rivers.* Boston: Ticknor and Fields, 1862.

Tunis, Edwin. *Beginnings of Early American Industry.* New York: Thomas Y. Crowell, 1957.

Ulrich, Laura Thatcher. *A Midwife's Tale: The Life of Martha Ballard, Based on Her Diary, 1785-1812.* New York: Alfred A. Knopf, 1990.

Ulrich, Laura Thatcher. *Goodwives: Image and Reality in the Lives of Women in Northern New England 1650-1750.* New York: Vintage Books, 1980.

Ulrich, Laura Thatcher. *The Age of Homespun: Objects and Stories in the Creation of an American Myth.* New York: Alfred A. Knopf, 2001.

Ulrich, Laura Thatcher, and Lois K. Stabler. "'Girling of it' in Eighteenth-Century New Hampshire," ed. Peter Benes. *Families and Children.* Boston: Boston University, 1985.

Webster, Noah. *A Compendious Dictionary of the English Language.* Hartford, CT: Sidney's Press, 1806.

Webster Word Histories. Springfield, MA: Webster, 1989.

Whitehill, Jane. *Food, Drink and Recipes of Early New England.* Sturbridge, MA: Old Sturbridge Village, 1963.

Willcox, William, ed. *The Papers of Benjamin Franklin*, Vol. 19. New Haven, CT: Yale University Press, 1976.

Wolf, Stephanie Grauman. *As Various As Their Lands: The Everyday Lives of Eighteenth-Century Americans.* New York: Harper Collins, 1993.

Young, Alfred F. *The Shoemaker and the Tea Party.* Boston: Beacon Press, 1999.

INDEX

rope key 52
rug 33, 34, 53

S

sad 128
Salisbury, Rebecca 29
salt 36, 37, 40, 50
Saponi 92
sauce or sass 49
scutch 23
scuttlebutt 104, 105
seamstress 24
set the table 51
settlers 2, 41, 43, 59, 64, 87
Sewell, Judge Samuel 111, 123, 126
shed 27, 31
shift 8, 63
shirt 65
short sass 49
shuffle-board 117
shuttle 27, 31, 119
silks 22, 25, 26, 59, 66
silversmith 5, 6, 11
skillet 37
slang 9, 48, 113, 128
slave 2, 13, 107
sleep tight 52, 53
smug 129
spider 37
spinster 27, 28
spoons 38
stage coach 130
stamp 92
Stamp Act 91, 95
stove 33, 53, 54, 57, 103
stump 8, 92
stump speech 92
sugar devils/sugar nippers 55
sugarloaf 55
sumptuary laws 59

T

tabby 68, 69
tablecloth 38, 63, 64

taken aback 105
talk turkey 129
tandem 16, 130
tarry 130, 131
tavern 3, 5, 7, 10, 38, 52, 71, 73, 76, 79, 80, 81, 82, 84, 85
tea 34, 75, 76, 77, 80, 85, 90, 95, 132
tea board 33
tea party 132, 140
tenter 28
tenterhooks 28
the third degree 131, 132
Thomas Jefferson 31
Thoreau, Henry David 5, 17, 139
thornback 29
tiffany 68
tinker 14, 15
tinker's damn (or dam) 15
tin ware 15
tip 125
toilet 33, 47, 48, 58
torpedo 132, 133
Tory 137
to the hilt 99
tow 21, 23, 29
towhead 29
trained bands 95
trammel 35
truck 15, 16
tumbrel 16
turnpike 116

U

U.S.S. John Hancock 104

V

velvet 24, 59
Vernon, Admiral Edward 78, 79
virgin 5, 30, 133

W

waistcoat 24
wallet 16, 17
warming pan 56, 57

ABOUT THE AUTHOR

 Joan Bines received her BA from Brandeis University and her doctorate from the University of Virginia in American diplomatic history. After teaching for many years, she became the director of the Golden Ball Tavern Museum, a gracious 1760s Georgian tavern and home in Weston, Massachusetts. Here with a dedicated group of volunteers, she oversaw and continues to oversee the preservation of the museum and to build its education and outreach programs. Here also, she has been able to indulge her love of words, their histories and meanings, as well as her love of photography.